Neglected Dimensions

Neglected Dimensions

Rough Sketches for Public Space

Paul Carter
(Text and Illustrations)

John Warwicker
(Book Design)

I.

My first
encounters with drawing
were atmospheric

In our humid
climate an awareness of lines in nature was a function
of the water cycle. Evaporation produced clouds, whose slow
choreography sometimes suggested writing in
motion. Condensation on window panes was a temptation
to draw shapes with a finger,
invariably causing the droplets to coagulate and strike
jerky clear paths to the bottom edge.
Left alone as winter's night came on,
these same fields froze into fractal patterns,
ferns,
flowers.
But the impressions left in the aftermath of rain
were most familiar: mud stuck to my boots and
caking off
preserved the stamp of my tread; mud inlaid with tyre and
bike tracks,
with
hooves and
paws.

Ours

was
clay
country

,

sticky underfoot where it clung
until one walked on stilts.
Oolitic limestone,
our vernacular building stone,
was little
more than petrified clumps of
shell. The field edges ran with
water; the river meadows tailed
off into cress beds;
the divisions
of our little town,
topographical and social alike,
were
the sculpture of drainage.

Sky-reflecting
pencils of water shimmering
like mercury,
rain-lodged grass,
flanks pale as silverpoint,
the burnish of storm
lash on trunk,
the distribution of
raindrops on the path,
and,
falling again,
typing itself
into puddles

My introduction to the culture of drawing was comic
Kneeling in the Methodist Chapel vestry,
my desk was an ancient wooden bench.
Trying to copy scenes from the Bible, my pencil got trapped in the grain of the wood; cross-hatching my little buildings or figures caused the patterning of the bench underneath to become visible. Developing inside my rude and unaccomplished Sunday School outlines was an accurate reproduction of weathered wood. One kind of drawing risked puncturing and laddering the paper, the other – a gentle, evenly spaced frottage or rubbing – caused an impression to come through alchemically. Later, the substitution of automatically reproducible patterns for any mastery of the image expressed itself in tracing maps, a process that involved retracing the negative image of the outline on the tracing paper's other side and, finally, laying the traced image on blank paper and, for a third time, tracing the outline. In this last iteration, the pressure of the pencil caused the graphite outline drawn on the underside to be impressed onto the blank sheet; but the impression obtained in this way was always variable and the outline discontinuous. In both cases, however, drawing was embraced as a way of letting nature draw back, a taste that, while it compensated for lack of independent technique or training, was consistent with the environment of impression-making and -taking in which I grew up.

Any visual training I had arose
from my passion for birds.
From primary school days I drew
passable profiles of the common species of the neighbourhood,
although mastery of their distinctive *Gestalten* was, I suppose, partly
due to copying illustrations in books. Convincing depictions of birds
in flight required a working knowledge of feather types and an
intuitive sense of the wind, derived in part from
observation and partly from the body memory of flying dreams.

Birds in flight were
also lines of flight:
the successful twitcher is a pacifist hunter,
and with his binoculars anticipates where the
fleeing bird will next break cover. Birds suggested
a point of view, the ichnographic
perspective of the aerialist
that is part of the fascination of ballooning
or sky-diving. In the fundamentally
enclosed corner of England where I grew up, their transcendence
of boundaries also suggested freedom; even within the confines
of coppice, garden or river side,
their accumulated evolutions marked out a creative region immune
to the laws of trespass. The famous Uffington
White Horse was close by
where I lived: the Chinese chalk brushstrokes used to
suggest its vaulting character, not to mention its beak,
suggested a dragon-like bird rather than a horse.
This ancestral movement form did not represent
anything, a local Pegasus anointing our local Mount Helicon,
say, it was a ground figure that inscribed choreography into
the view, annotating the natural slopes with a rhythmic signature.

Does anything from
this attenuated graphic heritage carry over to
the thought meanders, imaginary landscapes and
volumetric doodles reproduced in this book? Years of wandering in
the churches and piazze of Italy filled my mental gallery with
memorable images and compositions, and to fix their
complex arrangements
of windows and porticoes I made many notebook sketches; but no
gift for imitation is evident. Later, Aboriginal rock art and sand
drawing was a revelation because it integrated

the haptic and the
eidetic, forms seeming to mediate between the touch
of the finger and the texture of the world. Common to these different
landscapes was the the deferral of finish also found in the baroque
with its taste for over painting and the abstraction of the
arabesque. I liked the cultivation of the surface,
the impression of a luxuriant garden growing inside
the frame of a generally unsympathetic authority.
Cartographers filled up the expanses
of unfinished seas with
banderoles of script;
sculptors captured
in the hems of angels'
garments the self-organising
turbulence of breaking waves. The almost genetic
self-division, mutation and recombination of forms suggested that
a creative region could be carved out inside the view.
Attention to detail disclosed a desire of self-realisation and implied
a poetics of passage, the continuous production
of possible places that resisted the template of conformity and
the thin tyrannies of their graphic representation.

Public
place
was
not
given:

it was tunnelled out by bodies in flight
and the associations they formed,
an idea reinforced by my own passion for sports.
The historical connection between passion,

passing,

passage

and the physical footstep

caught in the French *pas* expressed my own sense that

place was inseparable from its performative production.

Later, I came across the novelist Robert Musil's meditation
on passion, delivered through the character of Ulrich
in *The Man Without Qualities*. Passion may seem to be 'something with
a way and a nature of its own. But, however completely
understandable and self-contained it seems,
it is accompanied by an obscure feeling that it is merely
half the story.' The other half of the story is 'a blind space,
space cut off behind all
the fullness.' This space is not empty. It is, as I noted
in *Meeting Place*, solid, like stuff, like Aristotle's *hyle* or matter.
It encases the individual as wood contains a worm: 'A wall is
formed by what is still to be lived and what has been
lived, and in the end his path resembles that of a
worm in the wood.'[1] The wood writing of ants and beetles,
exposed when bark is stripped or a rotten trunk splits open, is an apt
image of a drawing that is blindly sociable and nurtures
itself from the exploratory path it makes. The labyrinth
that forms when all these wandering lines intersect is not necessarily
claustrophobic: it may simply counter the sense of being lost
experienced in most cities,

Robert Musil, *The Man Without Qualities*, trans E. Wilkins and E. Kaiser, London: Picador, 1988, vol 1, 216 and Paul Carter, *Meeting Place: the human encounter and the challenge of coexistence*, Minneapolis: University of Minnesota Press, 2013, 170.

a map,

albeit incomplete, drawn using what philosopher Emmanuel Levinas
(writing of the *Figures entrelacées* of Charles Lapicque) calls

'the line as ambiguity' –

'Lines rid
themselves
of
their role
as
skeletons
to
become
the
infinity
of
possible paths
of
propinquity.'[2]

Emmanuel Levinas,
'The Transcendence of
Words: On Michel Leiris's
Biffures,' *Outside the Subject*,
trans. M.B. Smith, London:
Athlone Press, 1993, 145.

2.

Public space does not exist.

It is given –
or,
where
withheld,
wrested
from those
who deny it

with the threat of violence.

It is like a clearing in the forest, which is usually
the vestige of ancient industry, and whose maintenance
depends on diligent woodsmanship. Paths have to be made to and
from it, and they, too, have to be marked and maintained.
If its promise of emancipation is not to destroy us,
a rapprochement with the forest is necessary. The forest
is also public space and our alienation from it is due to a prior
alienation or historical enclosure that forced us collectively out of it.
State benevolence in these matters is always
secondary. In jurisdictions governed by the myth of crown land,
the physical distribution of what is metaphysically bestowed
on human kind involves a primary privatisation: what the
government does not retain for its own purposes is partitioned out
to powerful, private interests. The economic merits of the Enclosure Acts
may be debated, but the destruction wrought to sociability
is beyond dispute. The labourers who seemed, as William Cobbett
put it, to have been 'swept off the fields by a
hurricane,'
and who 'had dropped and found shelter under
the banks on the roadside,'3

William Cobbett, *Rural Rides*, London: T. Nelson & Sons, 1923, 19.

were legally no different from
the Dharug people to the west of Sydney who, thrown off their land,
'independently range the Woods in the day,

like the fowls of the air

or the beasts of the field,

and lie down in the Bush wherever night

overtakes them.'4

L.E. Threlkeld,
*Australian Reminiscences
& Papers*, ed. N. Gunson,
Canberra: Australian Institute
of Aboriginal Studies, 1974,
vol. 2, 347.

In England,

the Enclosure Acts overlaid feudal land arrangements:

in the resulting palimpsest of competing land claims,

some 'commonable waste' survived, usually under government

protection. In Australia, where pastoral expansion was not inhibited

by traditions of folkland, the surveyor's grid reversed
the principle mentioned before: it *remetaphysicalised*
the land as the physical roads into the country
were identified with the grid lines of the
survey. In the United States, where the myth of crown ownership

was jettisoned, this confusion of line and lane produced the

results described by A. R. Wallace: 'there are no roads or
paths whatever beyond the limits of the townships,
and the only lines of communication for foot
or horsemen or vehicles of any kind are along []
rectangular section-lines, often going up and down
hill, over bog or stream, and almost always
compelling the traveller to go a much greater
distance than the form of the surface rendered
necessary.'[5] In England, where road building was a branch

of civil engineering originating in military manoeuvres,

communication was improved – but taxed. Those who declined

to enrich the private turnpikes kept alive the old networks – in a 327

mile circuit made in 1822 to survey agricultural conditions in four

of England's southern counties Cobbett boasted, 'I have crossed
nearly the whole of this country ... without going
five hundred yards on a turnpike road, and,
as nearly, as I could do it,

in a straight line.'[6]

Alfred Russel Wallace,
My Life, New York: Dodd,
Mead & Company, 1905,
vol. 2, 192-193.

Cobbett, *Rural Rides*, 78.

When public authorities wrested back

public land in the public interest, they focused their attention tactically and strategically on land that was either central to communicational infrastructure or marginal to private economic interest. The object was to re-centralise spatial resources that had been de-centralised: perpetuating a system of land alienation that excluded the democratic voice, they regarded the retrieved public space feudally: 'in the public domain, accountability can come only through the Voice – in other words through argument, discussion, debate and democratic engagement. But in nineteenth- and early-twentieth-century Britain, accountability through Voice was lacking or attenuated; and the growth of the public domain did nothing to enhance it.'[7] At the core of the Gladstonian central state lay a tradition of autonomous executive power, a parliamentary monarchy which 'was not supposed to be democratic, still less participatory'[8] – one strong historical reason why the neo-liberal 'privatist renaissance' met so little public resistance.[9]

In an important sense the public has never become public

– never learned cosmopolitan virtues, respect for difference, intolerance of mystification, resistance to the usurpation of shared rights. Where democratic space remains

a phantom[10] or unrealized project,[11]

the retreat into self-interest is always imminent:

as Marquand observes, the individualism of market liberalism is

'in a profound sense private.'[12]

David Marquand, *Decline of the Public: The Hollowing out of Citizenship*, London: Polity Press, 2004, 61.

Marquand, *Decline of the Public*, 61.

'Democratic public space might, rather, be called a phantom because while it appears, it has no substantive identity and is, as a consequence, enigmatic.' Rosalyn Deutsche, 'Agoraphobia', in *Evictions: Art and Spatial Politics*, Cambridge, Mass.: The MIT Press, 1996, 269–327, 324.

Marquand, *Decline of the Public*, 92-3.

Deutsche, 'Agoraphobia', 180.

Marquand, *Decline of the Public*, 93.

Public space does not exist

as a discursive
domain – as
a place where
'language []
takes back its
lost wealth,'

and through the exchange

of ideas makes room for
things to happen.

Besides, as Guy Debord pointed out long ago, 'When it is controlled by power language always designates something other than authentic lived experience.' In the hands of planners, who, as a proxy of the state assume the right of '"unilateral" communication,' public space is an instrument of government, the enemy of all forms of insubordination (including that of words).[13] Instrumentalising everyday life in terms of the regulation of economic and social relations, it has confused relating with connecting and identified the latter with the prediction and satisfaction of stimulus-response associations. In Modernist design,

there is a direct relationship between
the enlargement of public space
and the extirpation of non-functionalist
forms of sociability. 'Man walks in a straight line
because he has a goal and knows where he is going;
he has made

up his mind to reach some particular place and he goes

straight to it.

The

pack-donkey meanders along, meditates a little in his scatter-brained
and distracted fashion, he zigzags in order to avoid the larger stones,

or to ease the climb, or to gain a little shade;

he takes the line of least resistance' – thus Le Corbusier,

whose lingering prestige in architectural circles

never ceases to amaze me.[14]

References in these lines are to Guy Debord, 'All the King's Men,' *Internationale Situationniste*, No.8, 1963, reprinted in *The Incomplete Work of the Situationist International*, ed. & trans. C. Gray, London: Free Fall Publications, 1974, 76-77.

Le Corbusier, *The City of To-Morrow and its planning*, trans. F. Etchells, Cambridge, Mass.: The MIT Press, 1971, 11.

The prejudice expressed here is not
strictly spatial but psychological; Le Corbusier proposed
the eradication
of the kind of tracks Cobbett took not because they were
crooked,
multiple
and
indefinitely marked (perhaps
a convenient myth) but because they represented
physically
resistance to progress.
The archetypal traveler of these routes,
prone to conversational backtracking
and poetic aside
was the Greek *agoraios* or
haunter of the agora; in future, such gypsy gymnasts of the
public domain would be driven out.[15]

Paul Carter, *Repressed Spaces,
The Poetics of Agoraphobia,*
London: Reaktion Books,
2002, 125-126.

Le Corbusier imagined the re-militarisation of the countryside:

'Once you get far enough
from the towns
you feel on solid ground again,
far from the city's unbelievable follies.

                  The main roads stretch

                        straight

                          to the horizon

                             ,

leading quite definitely from point to point ...'[16] Le Corbusier, *The City of To-Morrow and its planning*, 11.
But here (apropos of 'follies' in their sylvan sense) his metaphors let him
down:

        'On either side of your road there branch off

      winding roads for special purposes – roads for cattle, donkey

      tracks, roads for horses and for every imaginable thing. On the

      one hand there is a clear and definite intention, and on the other

      a rather clumsy compromise. We might compare it with the sap

      which rises straight up the tree and the casual way ... in which

            branches stretch out towards the light.'[17] Le Corbusier, *The City of To-Morrow and its planning*, 201, note 1.

We might, or we might reject this Cartesian nightmare,

             pointing out the network of chreodes

that form an 'epigenetic landscape'

    of hills

    and valleys,[18] See Scott F. Gilbert, 'Diachronic Biology Meets Evo-Devo: C.H. Waddington's Approach to Evolutionary Biology,' *Integrative & Comparative Biology* 40, 5 (2000): 729-737. At http://icb.oxfordjournals.org/content/40/5/729.full

admiring the irregular non-Euclidean geometry of trees,

               their branches

   and leaves

    and acknowledging the existence of the levitational force

impelling the tree's sap to move 'in an approximation

to a cycloid-spiral space-curve.'[19] Jane Cobbald, *Viktor Schauberger: A Life of Learning from Nature*, Edinburgh: Floris Books, 2006, 32.

   Le Corbusier's unawareness of self-organising systems and his

   mistaking of complexity for confusion can hardly be held against

   him. His significance lies in the fact that the deterministic

   thinking he exemplifies continues to be orthodox in urban

   planning and commercial development a century later.

It also continues

to characterize the dominant, government-patronised mode
of public space production with the result that an adequate
description of what is entailed is, at least in political and

administrative discourse,

encompassed by a few straight lines on a blank page.
To counter this dessication, at once mental and environmental,
a humid representation has been advocated, one that adapts the
features of colloidal systems in nature - clouds,

rainfall,
smoke,
mist,
blood   and
milk

are all colloids – to the description of
designed environments.
The Russian-German chemist Wilhelm Ostwald had described
colloids as

'lying in the World of Neglected Dimensions,' and in

Dark Writing I discussed how this world suspended between
bulk and molecular dispersal could be drawn, and the drawings
serve as richer descriptions of places than designs
usually allow. Colloids tend to form tracks and junctions;
to exhibit beautifully and irregularly stepped structures;
to proliferate surfaces that are rough and irregular;
to generate ooze forms,
or process forms - serpentine
or meander forms are process forms -

straight lines reflected
in undulating water also exhibit this property.

When scaled up, I wrote, in the context of the Melbourne Docklands development, their interwoven strands resemble the fisherman's net. With a radically non-linearist, humid redrawing of the public domain in mind, I compared the net's nodal points to the pilings driven into the silt that distribute the weight of the wharf. Noting that common to all these structures is the dispersal of weight, I presented some process drawings that tried to evoke the place as a trembling movement form, a self-organising field composing and recomposing itself in the feedback between choreography and topography (FIGS 1-9).[20]

Paul Carter, *Dark Writing, Geography, Performance, Design*, Honolulu: University of Hawaii Press, 2008, 177-182.

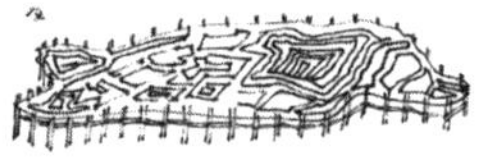

The drawings, sketches, doodles or graphic caprices collected here place the Victoria Harbour descriptions in context. Characterised as a representation of place from the point of view of flow, those images of architectural edge forms, or navigational analogies between the constellations of the sky and the arrangement of figure and ground (FIGS 10-11) were project-specific but drew on a modest lexicon of graphic forms used to evoke the neglected dimensions of public space as such.

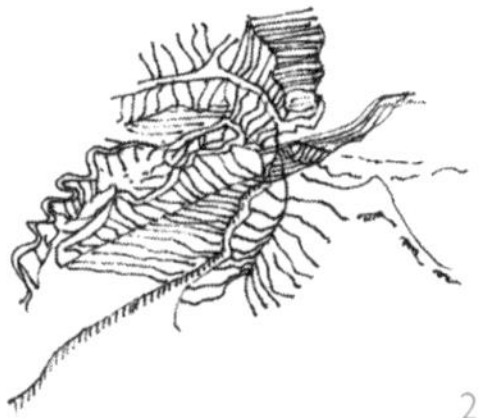

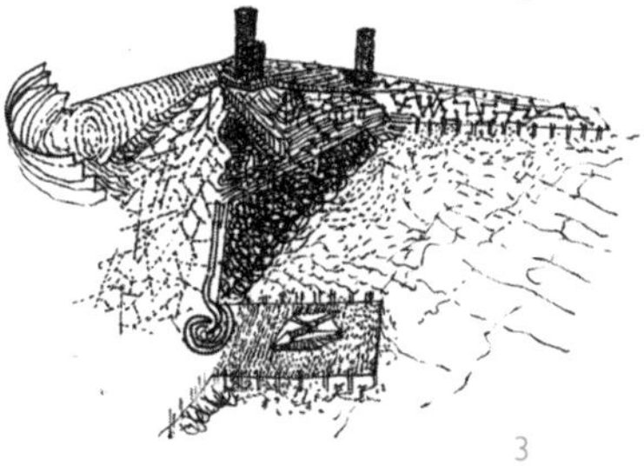

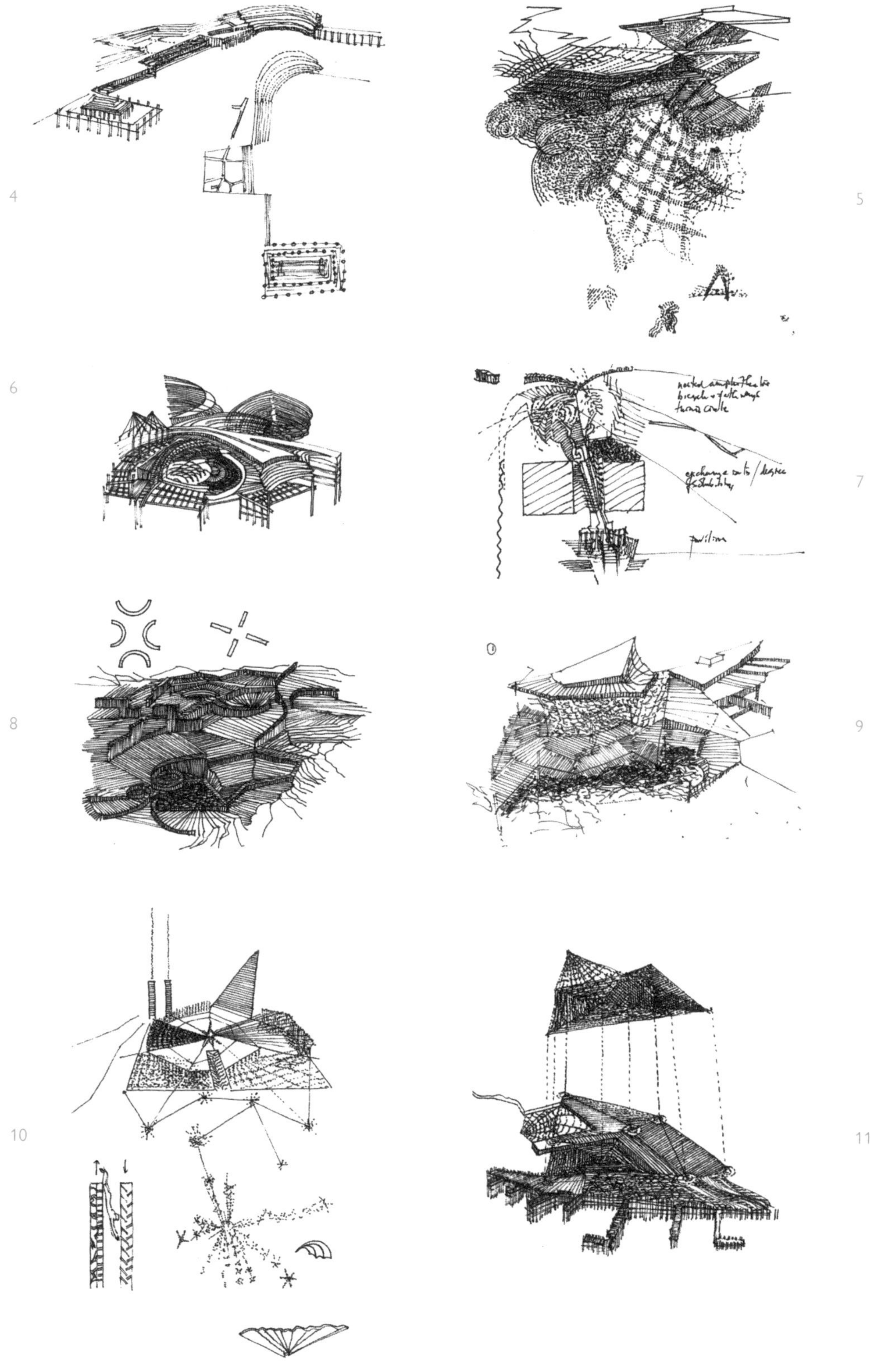

Public space does not survive as an abstraction:

envisaged apart from a situation that acts as the catalyst of social, environmental and political becoming-at-that-place, it is an administrative placebo. Like the behaviour of the self-organising crowd, it cannot be reduced to a formula. This is why all the *esquisses* presented here arose in direct response to place-making invitations; they collaborate with physical and human situations, whose intelligence and plastic creativity they draw on in their drawing. As the public space design opportunities that fell in my path arose from planning cultures that share views about the nature,

purpose,

design and regulation of public

space, the sketch designs have much in common with one another. The exploration of neglected dimensions of socio-spatial feedback – later I referred to this art of design as

choreotopography –

operated reactively, but in relation to the boundaries set by the institution or community inviting my work. For these reasons, certain movement forms –

resonant distributions,

turning points,

meeting places

and extruded gestures –

could be developed proto-linguistically from one situation to the next

;   they provided a kind of grammar or set of

possibilities.

If the sketches presented here
have any formal interest, it is due
to the fluidity of their syntax.
I want it to be clear that the linguistic
analogy needs to be taken with a pinch
of salt – not simply because the venerable
topos/topic analogy presupposes the
alignment of architecture with the
interests of those who hold power,
but because it implies a technique –
a command of draughtsmanship
and representational competence that
these drawings lack. It would be better
to compare these combinations
of lines, the ad hoc patchwork of their
patterning, to the contact jargons and
proto-Creoles improvised along the
margins of empire, where a system of
chance homologies and fertile ambiguities
sustains communication

rather than the

exchange of clearly defined and translatable
concepts. The syntax of these pre-lingual languages
is distinctively superficial: it does not well up from firm
grammatical
foundations but depends on a certain poetic disposition and
performative brio, as the chance recognition of convergent interests
dictates and mimetic hybridisation transforms one motif into
another. What counts in these fluid situations
is less the stability of the concept or image
than its power to generate connections; here
its primitive simplicity denotes a potential for combination, for
fragmentation and reconstruction. Attention is
drawn to the invisible forces of separation and
reunion that underwrite
the new order immanent in the apparent chaos.

Talking of the rules of writing, one other preliminary point can
be made: many of the earlier graphic arabesques are reproduced
from writing notebooks – from lined pages dotted with hand-
writing. There is a dance-like
relationship between
writing and drawing,
between the cursive hand
and the
calligraphic
impulse (FIG 12).

12

Three-dimensional letters are often incorporated into the
sculptural field of the drawing; or they may lie secreted
in a landscape like its geological anatomy (FIGS 13-15).

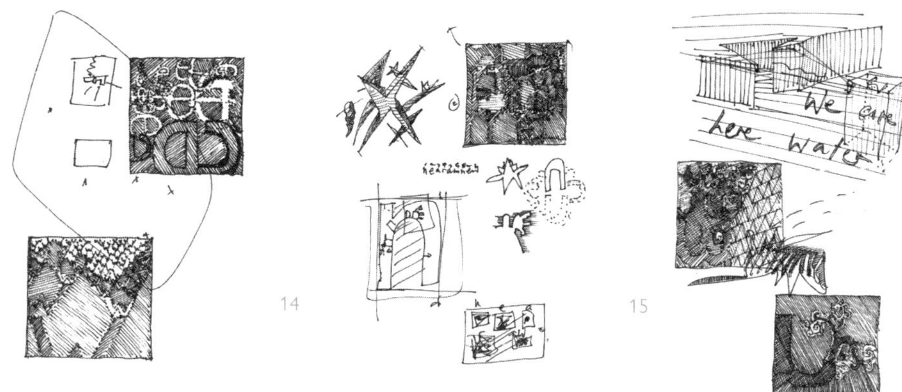

13 14 15

In other words, these sketches are never pure exercises
in visualisation; they are discursive diagrams, sifting the conventions
of one system of conceptualisation for their indexical residue.

I never thought that letters or phrases would be
representations of the objects they name or that
calligraphy directly illustrated an idea; but the internal
construction of the letter, and perhaps the trace it retains of hand-eye
coordination
(and beyond that of the 'cycloid-spiral space-curve'
that also characterises walking),

intrigue me. The mere act of drawing out records an
accumulating history of
passages; when the materiality of the mark is granted
value, attention passes from the metaphysical enclosure two lines
delineate to the relationship between the tracks. Then the avenue
of space between the lines is no longer privatized; it
becomes, instead, the space in-between whose evolution,

care and crossing is inseparable
from its first, mimetically-achieved recognition
across
the   gap.

3.

Solution grew out of two earlier projects: *Tribute*

and

Tracks

had in common an exploration of edge conditions. Doodles from these projects illustrate coastal transitions (promontories, inlets), erosion landscapes (incipient canyons, overflow deltas or headlands) and landscape design responses to these dynamic conditions (terraces, paths and stabilized recesses or basins) (FIGS 16-19). The focus on marginal environments reflected a tempcramental affinity and a biographical datum: they are political landscapes where the geometry of enclosure has broken down; as overflow regions of passage, of appearance and disappearance,

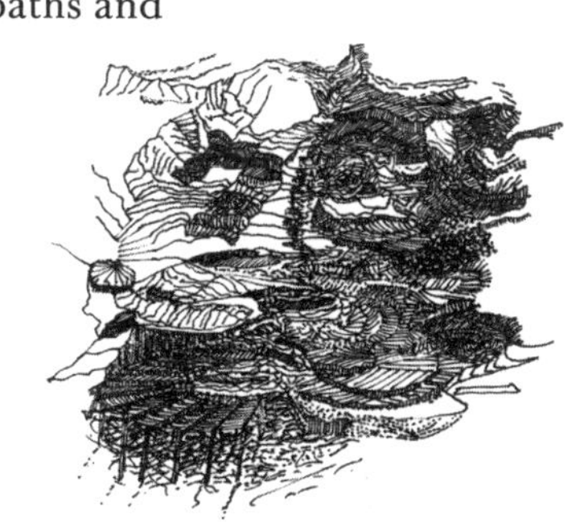

16

they are migratory zones.

Looking back,

I see that the situations

I chose

to study reflected my own professionally marginal position.
None of these designs was solicited or ever enjoyed official
approval; if acknowledged at all, they were classified as the
free environmental association of a public artist whose *techne*,
such as it was, consisted in poetic composition and
public space inscription. But from my point of view,
it is obvious that from the beginning I realized that
the matrix wrote back: erosion was
large-scale *écriture*,
and underwriting the terraces of the Muses
were diluvial
traces preserving older histories.
The original impulse behind the work that became
Nearamnew at Federation Square was a proposal
to give sculptural expression to an Aboriginal account of the
making of the place where Melbourne now stands. The story
was in two parts: first, Bunjil, the creator deity of the Kulin
nations, made the earth, cutting it in many places to form
creeks, rivers, mountains and valleys; then,
later,
when the men and women
he had created became very wicked,
he cut them up into tiny pieces,
and conjuring up whirlwinds of great force,
he dispersed these pieces all over the earth.

The tool he used to scar the earth and slice up the people was called

Ber-rang,

and it had the

unusual property of being able to 'open any place or any thing,

and in such a way as to make it impossible for anyone to know how

or whether or not it had been opened.'[21]

In 1990, a decade earlier I had tried to

realise the vortical force of the second creation

acoustically,

in a work called *Mirror States*[22];

associating the

Aboriginal 'dispersion of mankind' with the Tower of Babel myth,

I imagined
the whirlwind giving birth
to the mutually unintelligible
languages
of the world;

now the turbine of words
we had created sonically would be

a *wordcoil*

physically embedded in the Federation Square
landscape, the multilingual chaos
of the second (federal)

constitution of society represented as letters

drawn out of the surfaces

of the

place.[23]

[21] R. Brough Smyth, *The Aborigines of Victoria*, Melbourne: The Government Printer, 1876, 2 vols., vol. 1, 423; also Paul Carter, *Mythform, The Making of Nearamnew at Federation Square*, Melbourne: Carlton, Vic.: Miegunyah Press, 2005, 18.

[22] Paul Carter, *The Sound In-Between*, Sydney: UNSW Press/New Endeavour Press, 1992, 93-114.

[23] Carter, *Mythform*, 13.

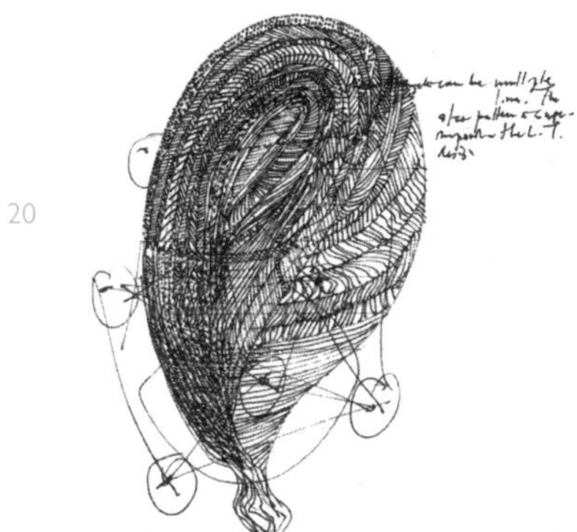

One outcome of this idea   was the set of line drawings
of

loops

that evolved into *Nearamnew*:
a global **whorl** pattern
     in which **whirl** rafts of sculptured lettering –
one   of which gives graphic expression
to   the story of the original scattering over the earth,
     others of which materialize into images
         of genital passage
             and rebirth (FIGS 20-22).

Although the whorl pattern found
expression, these movement form
variants remained sketchbook
speculations.[24]

The sequence of digital drawings in which the whorl form was tested and evolved into an interlock of fields is illustrated in *Mythform*, see, 18-20.

Indeed, many of
the notebook drawings
from that period largely relate to other, unfulfilled components
of the project.

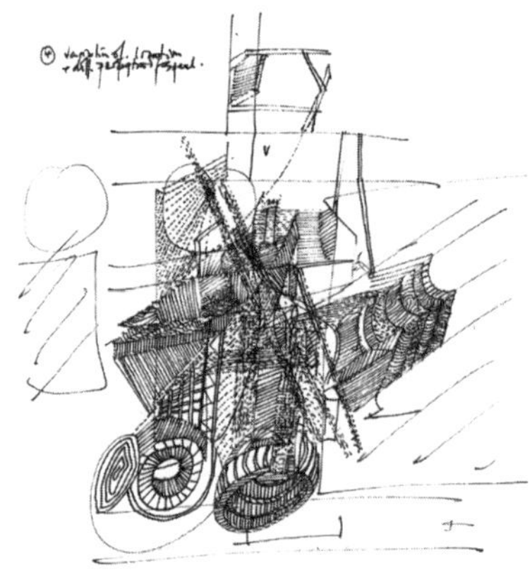

23

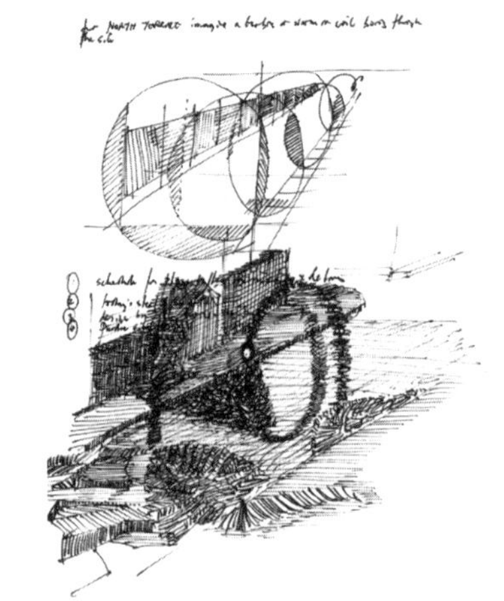

24

It is forgotten now that the plinth-like isolation of Federation Square from its immediate urban setting is a result of late government fiat. It was not part of the original intention (or expectation), which was to have the spaces of the new meeting place spill over the edges of the site and cross the banks of the Yarra into the river. In the context of this original ambition, the proposal to build a wordcoil, conceived as a cut-away Archimedean screw, its base in the water, its top at plaza level, was plausible (FIG 23) – a version of this was subsequently explored in *Tracks* (FIG 24).

A peculiarity of the proposal was its desire to represent the turbine of creation negatively; that is, to treat the matrix of the site itself as pregnant with words, whose exposure occurred when landscape forms were cut into the surfaces. Inspired by the magical power of the *Ber-rang*, I imagined an opening where the matrix wrote back so that it was impossible to tell apart what had been created from the forces that had created it.

The global whorl form of *Nearamnew* was influenced by a depiction of revolving water found in a 19th century Aboriginal bark etching collected from near Lake Tyrrell in the Victorian Mallee.[25] Carter, *Mythform*, 19-20. As discussed in *Ground Truthing*, the extraordinary craftsmanship and detail of the etching, together with its collection, circulation and preservation in white colonial circles – the work ended up in the Museum of Victoria's collection – suggested that the Aboriginal artist consciously composed a work for European tastes; its value was to be found in the impact it had on colonial sensibilities.[26] Paul Carter, *Ground Truthing, Explorations in a Creative Region*, Perth: UWAP, 2010, 95-109.

Produced in the wake of a disastrous pastoral invasion, it documented forest destruction but also the persistence of Indigenous senses of place and associated social, religious and economic practices. It proposed a new translation between conflicted parties and constitutions.

Similarly, experimental landscapes sketched for Federation Square's spillage down
to the river explored
the choreographic value
of a meander form
uniquely found in the
so-called Batman Treaty

(FIGS 25-33).

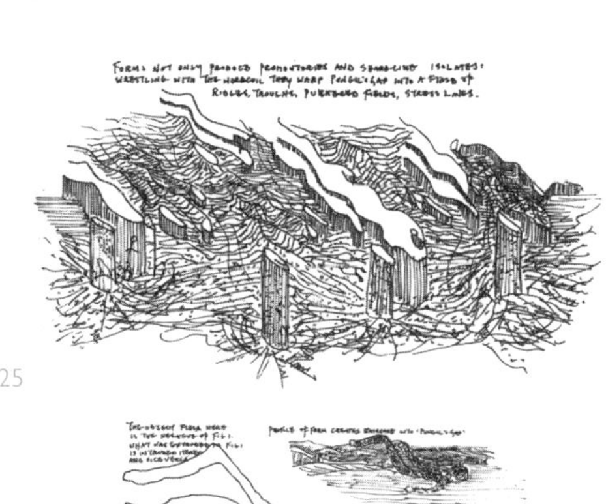

25

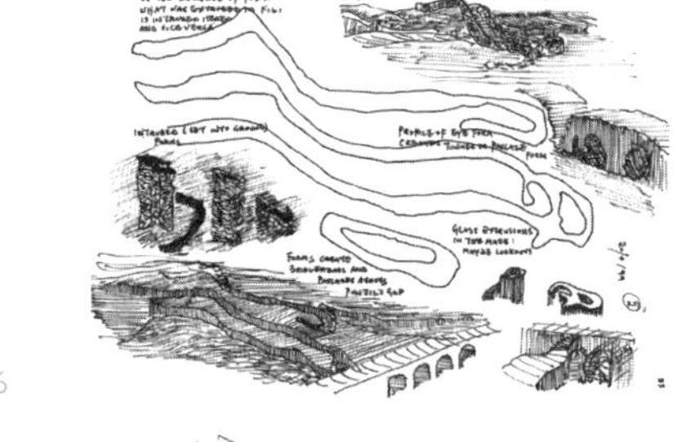

26

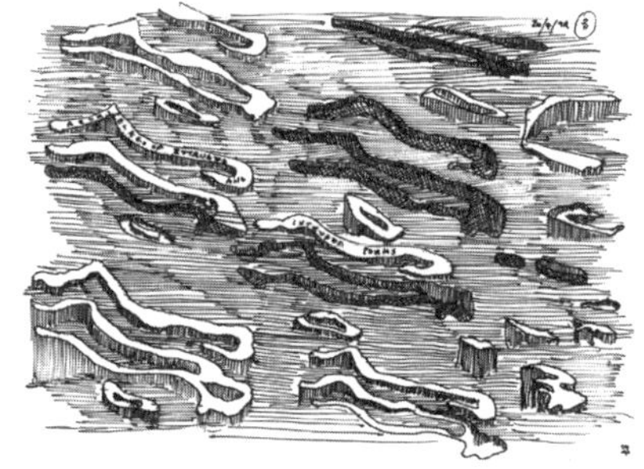

27

In the debate about the status of the conveyances John Batman claimed to have negotiated with eight chiefs 'who affixed their marks, or signatures, to the deed,'
I took a middle
position.[27]
While

James Dawson, *Australian Aborigines*, Melbourne: George Robertson, 1881, 112.

I thought that any
claim to legality must be spurious,
I doubted whether the documents were
pure inventions. I guessed that, however
cynical Batman's motivation may have been, the 'signatures'
appended to the documents were unlikely
to have been pure forgeries. As
authentic marks attached to an
inauthentic transaction, I construed them as
another attempt to reverse engineer colonial relations.

The author of *Australian Aborigines*, James Dawson, compared the signatures – sperm-like meanders, wavy silhouettes suggesting ghost figures reflected in flowing water – to marks Aboriginal people 'were in the habit of carving on the bark of trees and on their message sticks.'[28]

Dawson, *Australian Aborigines*, 112.

The allusion was to the famous dendroglyphs executed by the Wiradjuri people of central New South Wales. Tree writing of this kind has also been recorded in Victoria[29]; the conveyance meanders bore little resemblance to Wiradjuri/Kamilaroi tree carvings which, according to one early 20th century report were quasi-geometrical, physio- or

zoo-morphous.[30]

For evidence of funerary use in Boonwurrung country, see Marie Hansen Fels, *'I Succeeded Once': The Aboriginal Protectorate on the Mornington Peninsula, 1839-1840*, Canberra: Australian National University E Press, 2011, 272: Fig 33, 'Six monuments to the dead,' reproduces a sketch by William Thomas.

R. Etheridge, 'Teletoglyphs, or Bora-Trees' in *The Dendroglyphs, or "Carved Trees" of New South Wales*, Sydney: Memoirs of the Geological Survey of NSW, Ethnological Series 3, 1918, 59-91.

Perhaps Dawson had been led to this comparison by the mention of 'sinuous parallel lines and other marks on the trees' associated with the ceremonies of the Geawegal people of the Hunter Valley.[31] This comparison linked the Batman signatures to dendroglyphs and to designs inscribed into the inner surfaces of possum cloaks - a Victorian phenomenon.[32] While little is known about

See G.W. Rusdell, 'The Geawe-gal Tribe', 279-286 in Lorimer Fison and William Howitt, *Kamilaroi and Kurnai*, Melbourne: George Robertson, 1880, 279-286, 283.

A connection made by the curators of *Aboriginal Australia*, Sydney: Australian Gallery Directors Council, 1981, 34.

the meaning of the dendroglyphs, the cloak designs are thought to be 'representations or maps of the district from which the wearer came.'[33]

Aboriginal Australia, 35.

Then, I thought, the conveyance meanders might also be types of ground writing; *non-alphabetic letters* derived from the lie of the land. Next to each signature was a cross-hatched cloud drawn inside a square, a device that (on the analogy of similar designs found in possum cloak drawings) signified the country from which the signatory came. In the same spirit, I laid a crowd of Batman meanders (as if they were the people Bunjil cut this way and that with the *Ber-rang*) over the Lake Tyrrell etching (FIG 29).

Having explored the landforms that the Batman signatures might generate, I pondered the waterforms that might negotiate the gap between two systems of water management (FIGS 30-33).

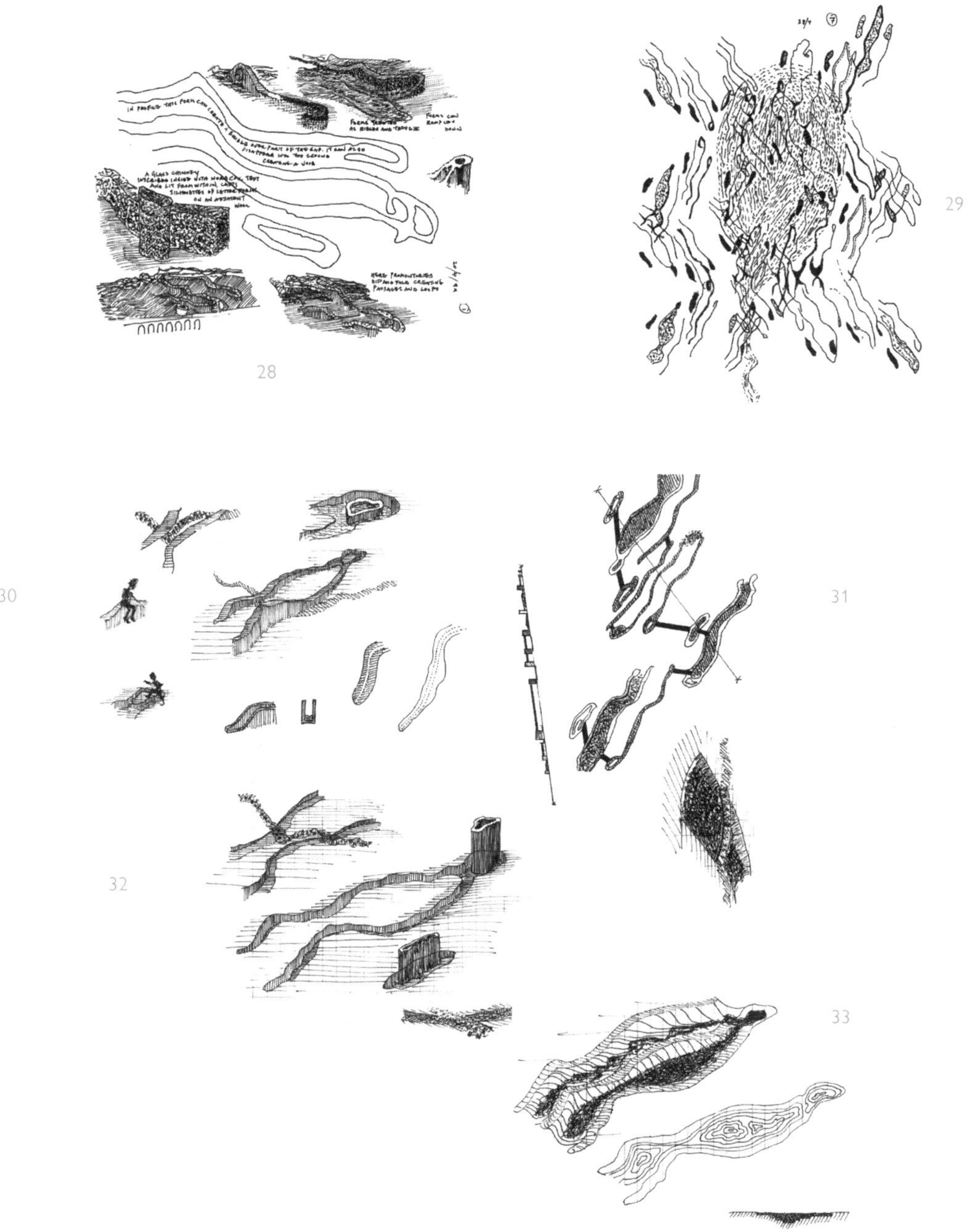

These place-making stories as writing –

as whirlpool,

whirlwind,

Ber-rang,

the invisible

openings and meanders – I interpreted
mythopoetically, as poetic mechanisms for *beginning
again* the process of self-becoming at that place. After
the cultural clear-felling of colonial history, they might provide the
initial conditions of real rather than symbolic reconstruction. The
territorial plague inaugurated by the Batman agreement led to poetic
as well as environmental dessication, destroying the creative
identification between society and setting – between the
self-organising imagination and the patterning of the
world. In that humid cultural environment, the European
distinction between moulding and carving had yet to become
axiomatic: the land forms Bunjil's *Ber-rang* cut could have been
kneaded out of clay. The same was true of people: 'The Melbourne
blacks say that PUND-JEL made of clay *two males.*' As regards the
site where Federation Square was now being built, in the 1840s, the
Assistant Protector William Thomas recalled: 'In company with some
blacks, I was looking at a brickmaker at work, near the new bridge
over the Yarra (Prince's Bridge), when a Western Port black, named
"Billy Lonsdale," seeing the brickmaker smoothing the clay in the
mould, said,

"Marminata, like 'em that PUND-JEL make 'em Koolin".'[34]

Carter, *Mythform,* 49
& 89.

In late 1998 describing *Extruded,*
a landscape concept or object field inspired by the signatures of
the chiefs (which later became *Tribute*), I explained,
'it is a peculiarity of the site that its foundations sit in a semi-liquid
matrix (of Coode Island silt) which tends under pressure to rise
rather than settle. There is not only a downward pressure of imposed

buildings, but a tendency of the lie of the land to counteract this
pressure and overflowing under it to raise it again.'[35]

Paul Carter, 'FEDacoustic, a proposal to create a federated suite of works, December 4, 1998,' 1-10. Unpublished.

In *Solution* I envisaged the entire public space in terms of silt's
generative, shape-forming intelligence.[36]

Carter, *Dark Writing*, 173-202.

Here, however, the object was sculptural: the design
expression of the creative turbine that had
driven scattered human kind to their new places,
inaugurating a federal society, was a hollow or turbulent passage
known as Bunjil's Gap; and wherever the invisible, gap-making
Ber-rang cut this way and that way, it exposed (extruded or
intruded) the signatures of the place. In this conception no
distinction was made between the place-making forces and the traces
they left: the glyphs,

        marks,

        scars,

        signatures or letters

were sculptural stabilisations of the vortex. They bore the imprint
of passage; they were movement forms. In the novel fragment
Die Lehrlinge zu Sais (The Novices of Sais), the German Romantic poet
and philosopher Novalis wrote about 'nature's own language' -
'that great cipher which we discern written everywhere, in wings,
egg-shells, clouds and snow, in crystals and stone formations,
on ice-covered waters,
on the inside and outside of mountains,

        plants,

        beasts,

        men,   in the lights of heaven.'[37]

Editors, 'Introduction: The Age of Reflexion' in *Romanticism and the Sciences*, eds. A. Cunningham and N. Jardine, Cambridge: Cambridge University Press, 1996, 6.

Influenced by D'Arcy Wentworth Thompson's *On Growth and Form*,
I assumed that the ciphers were simply the forming principle
of matter as such - not written into matter

                        but material

thinking.

Sketches done in April 1999 explored different extrusions and combinations of the meander signatures, Pungil's Gap (sic) and the multiply-braided whorl form derived from the Lake Tyrrell bark etching (FIGS 34-37). Different slopes, or transitional zones between the Federation Square deck and the Yarra-edge vaults under Princes Bridge, were imagined as interlocking systems of terraces,

                                         defiles,

                                         ridges

and   troughs.

Unhampered by conventional landscape design typologies and expectations, these sketches sought a recognition factor, an interface between the free-flowing object fields derived from the scripture of creation and the functional repertoire of bridges,

                              paths,

                              stairs

and   walls.

A feature of these complicated terrains is the clustering of wand-like figures, tree profiles or wavy stelae: oneiric, dendromorphic, they undulated like pages designed for water writing. In a second series, dating from early October of the same year, intrusions were derived from the meander forms, which were imagined as channels or systems of anastomosing billabongs. Allusion was made to the ancient form of the Yarra wetlands; I was attempting to materialise the hollow as a movement form; hollowing the earth, transporting silt from one place to another to form

    sandbanks,

    meanders,

    ox-bows and eddies,

    active water,

    cycloid,

    spiral,

    like *Ber-rang*, combined carving and moulding

    (FIGS 30-33)

       •

4.

The elaborate conceptual background just described

may seem to be out of proportion to either the quality or the quantity of the graphic yield.

Besides, neither *Extruded* nor its watery successor *Tribute* ever got to the planning stage. However, I have risked providing some depth of context because the ideas I explored around the periphery of the new Federation Square were generative. The strategies devised for negotiating changes of state or edge conditions spilled over, as it were, into subsequent commissions, site investigations or design dialogues. A provocative instance of land-water reversal was the gap or basin proposed for the new Geelong Waterfront development in 2000.

In adapting the Lake Tyrrell whorl to the patterning of the
cobbles at Federation Square, I had pointed out a sky-earth analogy:
besides representing the occasional overflow of water into
Lake Tyrrell, the drawing was said to refer to the Greater Magellanic
Cloud.

Early travellers crossing the plain
between Melbourne and Geelong had similarly deepened and
heightened the seeming flatness of the country. Bland had said that
the ground 'presented frequent chasms, wide and deep,'[38]
while Hovell wrote that 'since approaching this Country
it has appeared to us as if we had suddenly been
transported from one Cloud to another.'[39]
Reconciling these different perspectives, I imagined a mould made
of the sky-touching Barrabool Hills, immediately to the west of
Geelong, inverted and recessed into the Waterfront (FIGS 38-39).

William Bland in *Hume and Hovell, 1824*. ed. A. E. J. Andrews, Hobart: Blubber Head Press, 1981, 66.

William Bland in *Hume and Hovell, 1824*. 217.

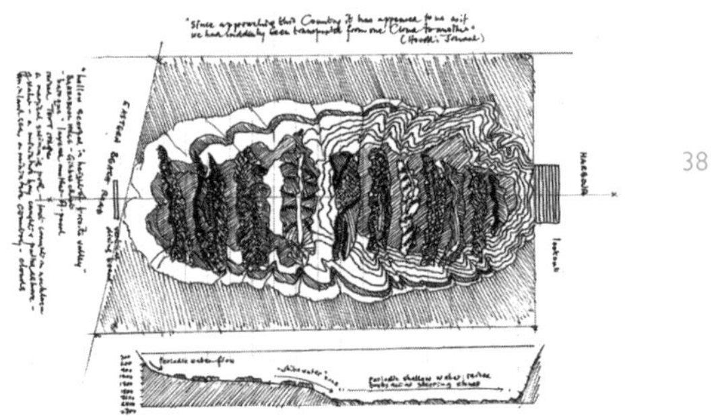

38

Overflow created a counterflow in the edge: interrupting pedestrian
passage parallel to the water,
it was not a chasm but a gap.
Periodically filled and outflowing,
its water rushing over
and through a sculptural
letter field
made figures writ in
water
legible.

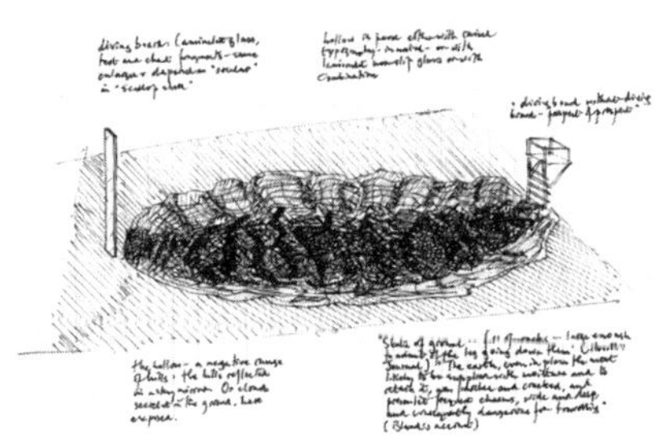

39

An oddity of *Overflow* was its reconstruction of the horizon.
In another version, the gap was drawn as a shard-strewn defile,
climbing out of the earth towards a typical swimming pool ladder:
reversing expectations, the ladder and diving board provided
a visual prospect of the bay but no physical access to it. They stood
for a sterile engineering tradition. At that time, I had begun my
studies of the Paestum Diver, a Greek Etruscan painting from the
early 5th Century BC; I was fascinated by the mirror image of
the diver in water and by the mystery of the transition; I wanted
to deepen the edge and reconfigure the shattering of the mirror
as a gradual transformation; in general, I wanted to restage
taken-for-granted traverses of the ground and reintroduce the
sensation of measure. The object was to intensify the drama of
encounter and reinstate, if you like, the step, in the double sense
of level change and stride. The shard-strewn walk of *Overflow*,
or the complexly tiered and hollowed sloping paths
of *Extruded* (FIG 37, for example) look on the face of it
impractical. They certainly would not meet Public Safety
Standards. Their design presupposed the existence
of an *eido-kinetic* intuition, an innate capacity to judge
distance, and to find pleasure in the
navigation of complex object fields.[40] ....

Carter, *Dark Writing*, 267-271.

It reproduced a sensation I had experienced a few years earlier
approaching an Aboriginal rock art site in the Grampians:

> 'there is no ground, no settled place among the jumble of fallen
> boulders, only an arrangement of curves, a transformational
> series of springing steps. No level places present themselves
> where one may stop, sit down and forget the body:
>
> each point of landing resembles the momentary pose
>
> of the dance,
>
> an in-between figure
>
> articulating motion
>
> not stasis.'[41] ....

Carter, *The Sound In-Between*, 135.

In a related series, stimulated by the invitation to think about the
design of entrance markers for Adelaide's North Terrace, I married
this idea to a sculptural interpretation of intentional traces – mainly
Indigenous rock art – collected and redrawn in scientific publications.
I wanted, as it were, to repatriate these marks to their three- and
four-dimensional environmental milieu.

In *Tribute,* the signatures were presented like
compacted debris. The exposure of the
matrix they formed was archaeological as fossil objects were carefully
exposed or patterns of stratification retraced. But what if markings –
scars,

    stencils,

    tracks,

    letter forms – were not jumbled together like a rubbish

                 heap

but were themselves generative: what if the landscape was
not derived from the accidental arrangement
and juxtaposition of ciphers but derived its form,
and grew out of, the markings themselves?
This was the thought experiment carried forward in *Tracks,* where
a selection of 'movement forms' was made and transformed
into three dimensional object fields (it was difficult to say whether
they were sculptural proposals or landscape designs) (FIGS 40-41).

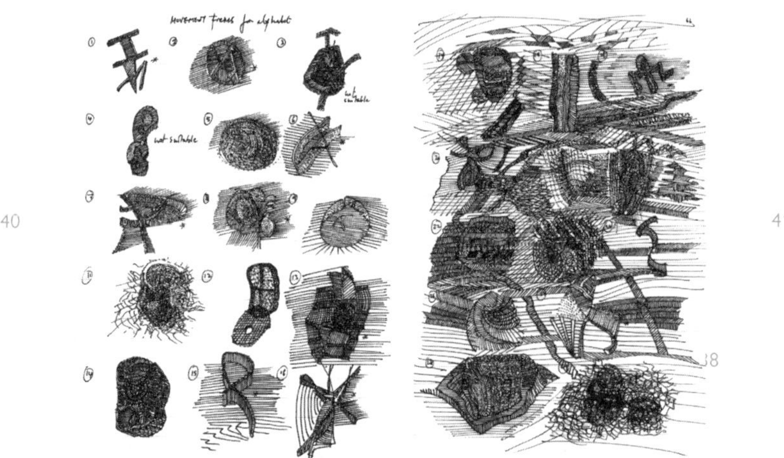

The background to this was the invitation to participate in the
redesign of Adelaide's premier street and townscape, North Terrace.[42]
One of

Carter, *Dark Writing*, 140-172.

my goals was to put the *terrace* back into a street that over the years
had become uniformly planar and divisionist. This involved
retracing the capillary action of a remnant humid environment
operating at right angles to the orientation of the street as well
as conducting a kind of archaeological dig for movement forms
repressed by the present planning orthodoxy of straight,

smooth and

featureless surfaces.

Besides the cairn studies and the iconographs, or movement forms
I also imagined Adelaide – the self-styled 'Athens of the South' -
as a vast classical caprice, set, perhaps post-earthquake,

into a Mediterranean landscape.

Sketches (FIGS 42-44) done between mid-November 1999 and
late July 2001 feature aerial perspectives of an entirely re-imagined
Adelaide. In these, buildings float like rafts in a tumultuous ground
swell of folded hills and valleys, stepped promontories; the thin
terrace of linear order emerges out of geometry's turbulent wreckage.

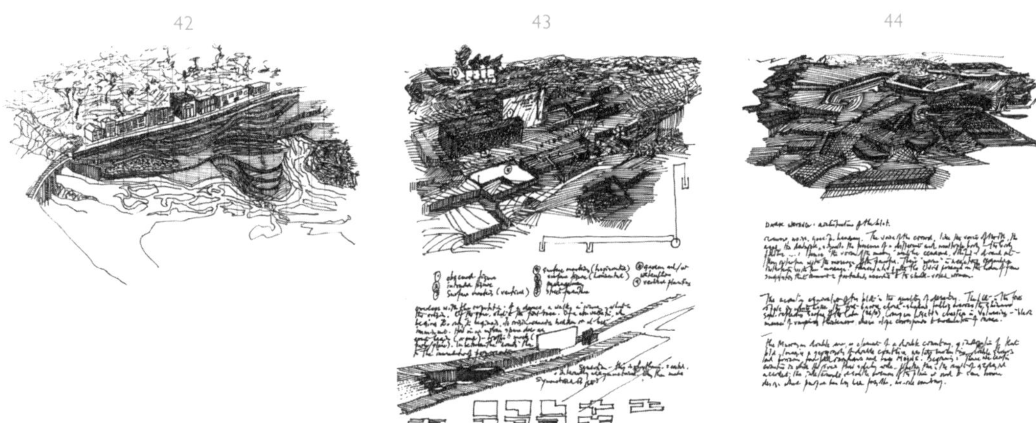

If architectural or urban forms predominate, they transfer attention
from stand-alone buildings to a strangely magnified and masterful
infrastructure of interlocking planes. The *Tracks* project overlapped
in time with *Solution* and a thumbnail sketch of a reconfigured
Victoria Harbour edge, integrating pile village platforms,
amphitheatre and terracing (FIG 6) from February 2002 clearly
transposes edge forms from the Adelaide
project back to Melbourne.

However, in understanding
the lattices, volutes and scaffolds
of *Solution*, another style of landscape
is important, one illustrated
in the immediately adjacent study FIG 45.

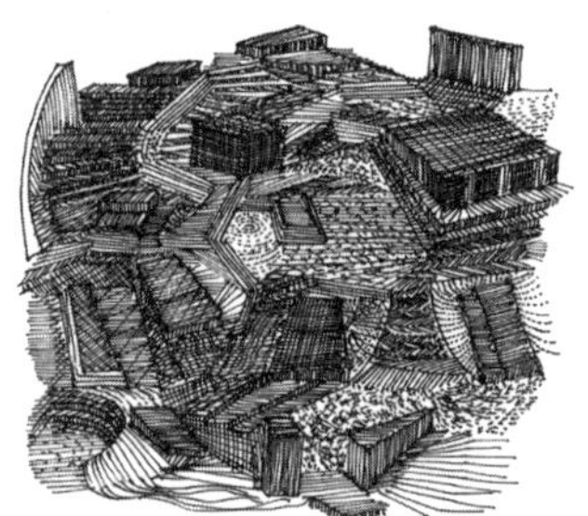

45

The first of these free landscape
improvisations is FIG 46, a cascading
pinball machine slope,
a maze of branching or convergent
courses

    and paths,

    sudden ridges,

    or rapids,

    or ranges of cliffs,

all eventually pouring into a vast
helically ramped basin in the
foreground.

46

Formally, it is a curious hybrid of *Tribute*,

        Overflow

and early *Tracks* studies.

Inverting the association of public space

with the provision of empty enclosures, it recalls its author
and designer, 'Eros, the Public Worker,'

and visualizes

'the erotic logic informing the empirical mass.' [43]

A number of similarly conceived urban landscapes followed:
(FIGS 47-50), done between July 2000 and late May 2003,
reintroduce the lie of the land into the consciousness of the modern
city. In *Repressed Spaces*, I pointed out the common origin of the terms
forum and *forest*; etymologically, both refer to outside places, where,
if you like, hidden desires are extruded, visualized or otherwise
enacted.[44] Forces of aggregation and disaggregation
struggle for dominance;

Carter, *Meeting Place*, 15.

the continuous production of sociability is inextricably linked to the erosion of the existing inhibitions to self·

47

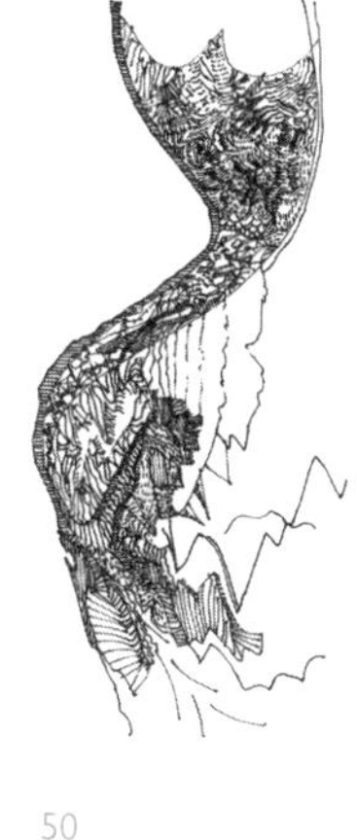

48

49

50

A composition of planes,
energetic frequencies,
inclinations,
visualises the production of space
dramaturgically, as a feedback loop
between the pen that draws (or the subject that passes through) and
the immediate environment. The hinging of slopes,
the evolution of spirals,
regions of landslide or
torrent,
or the emergence of
net-like linings
supporting the stretch and stress of the ground plane, these suggest
Ber-rang as the tool of sociability.

The history of tracks but also the counter history of erasure are tracked: blockages or unfulfilled expectations are part of the heritage. However, out of the turbulence of social endeavour emerges a field that,

however chaotically,
fits together
and faithfully expresses the performative logic of encounter
where the meeting of strangers does not necessarily lead to war
but can, instead, make room for something novel and interesting
to happen. In the sketches from the Australian notebook A35
a cellular landscape has almost wholly buried any sign of the urban
grid and it is a moot point whether anyone could live in these
postdiluvial flow fields.

In A35 (April 2003-July 2004) a new kind of doodle or graphic improvisation begins. In this, the perspectival or ichnographic representation of a possible landscape has disappeared and a field is depicted whose graphic elements grow,

combine,

evolve

and self-transform according to formal parameters defined by the field itself. Any representational illusion has largely gone; or, rather, instead of being imaginable as landscapes, these new designs inhabit a dream world of free formal association quite detached from real worldly concerns. At the same time, their earnest excavation of spaces internal to them suggests purposeful intent rather than the luxury of reverie; their patchwork of meanders,

cylinders,

lattices,

webs,

shards

and other organic and inorganic structural archetypes may be abstract, but it continues to suggest a fascination with composition as such. The equivalence of objects and spaces is assumed, and hence they can be thought of as descriptions of ambience.

Transitional in this regard is PLATE 1. The Adelaide iconographs had generated miniature landscapes from movement forms (fossil tracks, petroglyphs, etc): in this sketch for *Solution*, the same principle is applied to the generation of a movement place. Typically, the object is to represent the new place negatively, as a colloid system whose powers of combinatory self-organisation had historically been disparaged. Following my interest in writing and typography, where I also paid attention to the way missing letters and words might be indicated, I invented what I called the 'asterisk principle,' a way of marking absences in such a way

that they shone out
more brightly. PLATE 1 is a constellation or lattice of
asterisk-iconographs. I wanted to see what kind of field their
arrangement might produce.
Imagining the nodes as vibrating
regions,
I wondered what second order forms might emerge
from
their interference.

Although the new series (PLATES 2-16)
substitutes a graphic logic of composition for any perspectival
illusionism, the sketches remain tied to the investigation of specific
situations. The earlier sketches can be linked to places discussed
or visited: PLATE 2 was a contribution to the Botanic Gardens
of Adelaide Master Plan prepared by Taylor, Cullity, Lethlean
in November 2003; PLATE 3 was drawn around the sarcophagus
of King Seti in the Sir John Soane Museum.

In contrast, the writing
underneath PLATE 4 suggests that this sketch aims to describe

'an environment without genealogy.'

In fact, this interpretation links the three sketches, as they all seek
in different ways to visualize the initial conditions of places derived
from objects that, apart from their mere contiguity, have nothing in
common – certainly not a shared origin. In this sense they are
typically migrant aides-memoires, relying solely on what lies to
hand to yield up an order. Weaving different pattern scraps
into a continuous field, or interweaving different
motifs without regard to any prior organizational
template, they pidginize the picturesque. No visual
grammar exists to make the relationship of one part to another
legible.

No compositional syntax operates;
the different components desire of their own volition
to combine. In some drawings a string figure or lattice
is suspended from the corners like a hammock; while drawn to the
centre, it resists the confusion of parts piled up together, insisting
that the motifs sew themselves together without entirely losing
their identity.

A Botanic Garden where plant specimens collected in every
corner of the world thrive side by side illustrates a conception of
place as the active, ordering principle that enables unlike things to lie
side-by-side. Place fuses with placing; and placing, the
discovery of how and when things fit together
permitting access to a new domain, is the
experimental work of design. It is unlikely that the
elements of these doodles, primitive in themselves, could exist apart.
As memory places they are locative involutes –
'far more of our
deepest thoughts and feelings pass to us through perplexed
combinations of *concrete* objects, pass to us as *involutes*
(if I may coin that word) in compound experiences incapable
of being disentangled,
than ever reach us *directly*,
and in their own abstract states.'[45]

Thomas De Quincey, *Confessions of an English Opium-Eater and Suspiria de Profundis*, Boston: Ticknor, Reed, and Fields, 1866, 173.

Thus Thomas De Quincey, who also imagined the sum of all the
tracks made in the sea as an 'undistinguishable blot.'[46]

De Quincey, *Confessions of an English Opium-Eater and Suspiria de Profundis*, 214.

Images of perplexed combination are an X-ray of social metabolism;
entangled and morphed motifs suggest
a transformational transfer of energy
or the anonymous communication
of social desire.

Explaining the creative nature of memory, De Quincey writes that
a vellum palimpsest reused over centuries might well provoke mirth
because of 'the grotesque collisions of those successive themes,
having no natural connection, which by pure accident have
consecutively occupied the roll.' In the 'mighty palimpscst [of] thc
brain,' however, there cannot be such 'incoherencies.'

> 'The fleeting accidents of a man's life, and its external shows,
> may indeed be irrelate and incongruous; but the organising
> principles which fuse into harmony, and gather about fixed
> predetermined centres, whatever heterogeneous elements life
> may have accumulated from without, will not permit the grandeur
> of human unity greatly to be violated.'[47]

De Quincey, *Confessions of an English Opium-Eater and Suspiria de Profundis*, 233.

In a comparable way, some doodles gather irrelate and incongruous
themes about fixed predetermined centres, even if these are presented
in cryptic disguise. A second description of the Adelaide Botanic
Gardens
is richer in content and can be characterized as a fantasy taxonomy
in which motifs are substituted for species (PLATE 5). Adjacent notes
meditate on the garden as a refuge for threatened ideas,
drawing a parallel
between mental biodiversity and horticulture. But these are
processes rather than representations, histories of
pathways rather than maps.

Certain patterns or ordering
devices emerge: PLATE 6 hints at a cruciform structure – it is an
amalgamation of two memories, a perspective view of Adelaide's
North Terrace and cross-laid spars stacked in a pyramid – which
appears again, greatly strengthened, in PLATES 7, 8 and 14.

However,

any organising principle represented by these dimensionless lines is
weak: a jungle of meanders,

terraces,

dancing landscapes immediately colonises and

materializes them, creating corners,

knots,

masks

and tears. The offset

halves of an arch detectable in PLATE 6

refer to the proposal to create an 'entrance work'

at the west end of North Terrace

(the pyramidal structure just

mentioned was another cairn-style

way marker).[48]

Adelaide's primary designer, William Light,

was familiar with the neo-Baroque

city of New Noto in Sicily;

I recalled the archway leading

into that city. But much else

is conjured up to make a memory

landscape in the form of a patchwork

quilt, as if, by being bound together,

the fragments would remember
older unity and contiguity would

fuse them
into harmony.

an

[48] These as well as Plates 1, 2, 3, 4, 6 and 38 and Figs 5, 20, 38, 40 and 50 were shown in the exhibition sequence *Descriptions*, SASA Gallery, University of South Australia, October, 2003.

PLATES 9 and 15 imagine public space later.
The patchworks correspond to the Greek definition of chaos,
not as void or formlessness, but as the yawning, or gaping open,
of time and space to permit creation. Just as the Greek word *chaos*
can be linked to the term *chora* (meaning, very approximately, place)
– the turbulent masses of those doodles are dynamic. In the *Timaeus*,
Plato defines the *chora*, not as a 'receptacle of the forms' but as
'a complex movement' that involves 'movements both of the *chora*
and of the traces within the *chora*.'[49] John Sallis, *Chorology: On beginnings in Plato's* Timaeus, Bloomington: Indiana University Press, 1999, 126.
In a similar way, these two
sketches describe arrangements of public space *after* the traces
or *ichnoi* have fled to their proper places.

In Plato's model, the places are elemental – air climbs to the sky,
water runs downwards,
fire springs from the
bowels of the earth
and ravages the forest
and the earth sinks
down;
in our cosmology, the driving force is Eros, the Public Worker; the
elements are social beings that bunch locally and arrange themselves
regionally according to primary impulses of attraction and repulsion.
The drama of this double movement is the subject of PLATE 11 where
the sinuous wall that divides the forest provokes a desire of meeting.
In PLATE 13 the ground plane itself has melted,
creating walls everywhere – and their corollary,
a maze of pathways ingeniously relating the figures
across the abyss.

A recent visit to the Guggenheim Museum in Bilbao,
where I wandered through Richard Serra's *The Matter of Time*,
Franz Kafka's comment, 'If one builds such large squares only out of
arrogance, why not also build a stone railing that could lead through
the square,'[50] Harald Salfellner, *Franz Kafka and Prague*, Pragu: Vitalis, 1998, 76.
and a project called 'Save the Wall,' inspired by a theatre

production in Berlin: these are recognizable influences on PLATE 11
which, because of this, is unusually explicit.
The blackened trunks might be the Australian bush after fire. Alberto
Giacometti said that his stalking groups were inspired by the edges of
the Engadine pine forests[51] Carter, *Meeting Place*, 49.

                                – my sociable matchsticks
could recall this, bringing the forest into the forum

                                        in a rather literal way.

In an essay called 'The Chi Complex: the ambiguities of meeting,'
I discussed the Greek letter *chi* as a figure of crossing, not least
because the letter links chaos to the chora. I called *chi* the limping
figure whose vulnerability and dependence creates a difference that
elicits compassion. I thought of the *chi*'s unequal cross as the drawing
of encounter – 'Crossing and crossed, the eloquence of the line
is interrupted, and ambiguity installed as the mark
of communication … It is the introduction of measure into a world
whose worship of speed has overwhelmed rhythm.

                  It is the sign of withdrawal that advances.
It is, in short, one of the movement forms that unravels the enigma
                                  of meeting.'[52] Paul Carter, 'The Chi Complex: The Ambiguities of Meeting', CLC Web: Comparative Literature and Culture, 12.4 (2010), 1-9, 8.

The beginnings of this thought can be seen in the crossings of the
tree figures in PLATE 11 and in the exposed timber frames of PLATE
13 where the upright croziers are *chi* forms *manqués*, lacking the cross
stroke that would let them walk. Other sketches from this time
(FIGS 51-52) consist entirely of hooked *chi* figures.

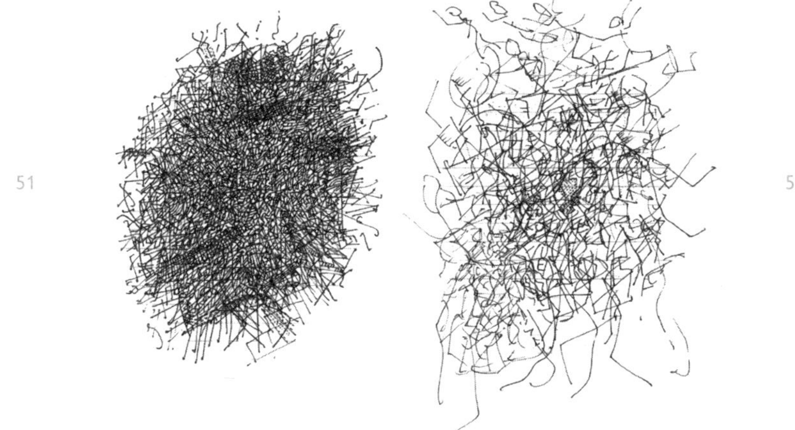

51   52

5.

The enigma of public space

emerges
when
we try to
define its
scale.

If scale, a sense of relative size, is a function of viewpoint, what happens when all the points of view count equally? If every vanishing point is someone else's viewing point –

if the equalisation of near and far is multiplied to encompass every
member of the public – any sense of perspective, and the hierarchical
ordering of public space it supports, are cancelled out. While the
planning authorities may fear a loss of control, speaking darkly
of lawless anarchy, the logical corollary of scalelessness

is anarchy

of a different kind, self-organising and chaotic in the ancient Greek
sense. Where measures of near and far no longer serve to discriminate
between oneself and others, the remotest figure – little more than
a pinprick on the horizon – and the companion at one's side loom up,
equally important.

The region of care presided over by Eros, the Public Worker,
embraces everyone equally; and every situation or encounter,
instead of being separated from the crowd, incorporates this larger
sense of belonging and compulsion. The horizon is *in your
face*; the face comes from its edges; its desire to be received turns
space (mere extension) into *chora* or *receptacle*. Public space conceived
dyadically or multiply consists of eddies, volutes and meanders.
It is like a vortex rather than a chequerboard.

In *Pine* (2004-2008), a project about Alberto Giacometti's sole public
art commission, a group of figures for Pine Street Plaza, immediately
adjoining the (then) new Chase Manhattan Bank in Lower
Manhattan, the obvious first question concerned the fact that the
artist never delivered the work. Maquettes exist, as well as
monumental bronzes of individual figures, but no serious attempt
was made to consider their effect in situ. Well after the commission
had stalled, Giacometti visited the site (for the first time) and,
according to his biographer, experimented with the arrangement
of human figures; stimulated by the dramaturgical insight this
yielded, Giacometti returned to Italy with the idea of creating one
or more figures on a far larger scale. However, his death intervened,
and the project lapsed.

Retracing the story, I became convinced that the major
problem that inhibited Giacometti was *scale*: how to relate his statues
to the size of the public space represented by Pine Street Plaza and
 its new skyscraper immediately adjacent. This thesis is fully discussed
in *Meeting Place*, and I won't repeat the argument.[53]
The point here is that *Pine* proposed to address the question of scale –
the relationship between the interior space defining the drama of
Giacometti's stalking groups and the exterior space of the outside,
inhabited by human beings absorbed in their own daily dramas –
through the device of *ladders*.

O riginally, *Pine* had been conceived in response to the 9/11
outrage – the situation evoked in PLATE 17. However, I draw attention
to that sketch in order to make a contrast: there is an obvious
resemblance between the ladder and the lattice – psychologically,
however, I have not imagined the ladder as cut out of the lattice but,
rather, anthropomorphically, as the human figure reduced to the bare
essentials of measure. The ladder stands like a tree
in the forest – related, certainly, but deriving its expressive
power from its standing,
    its stature, volume and disposition. In short,
dramaturgically-speaking, the ladder combines an internal space and
drama (measured in the relationship of the two vertical stiles and in
the rhythm of the rungs connecting them) with an external reach,
evident when the ladder is leant against a wall or used to scale a tree
– it is no accident that the Latin *scala* (ladder) and scale are the same
word for, essentially,

>the ladder is the measure of scale,
>
>the device that translates between
>
>the human stride and the unit

of public space.

Carter, *Meeting Place*,
196-205.

The significance I gave to ladders is evident
in a poem I wrote:

> They imagine the infinite in steps,
>
> They equivocate about depths and heights …
>
> Ladders are the evidence of unborn stairways,
>
> They are the thoughts that buildings repress;
>
> They feel like the copies of their shadows …
>
> The ladder is a structure of the beyond,
>
> The minimal equipment of transcendence …
>
> Between trees ladders grow, spreading wings.
>
> Ladders are half ladders fused together.[54]

Paul Carter, 'Ladders,' *Ecstacies and Elegies*, Perth: UWAP, 2013, 96-98.

The *Pine* project generated many ladder doodles (FIGS 53-55)
as well as Photoshop photomontages, exploring how the
transformation of Giacometti's figures into ladders might resolve
the problem of their dwarfing).

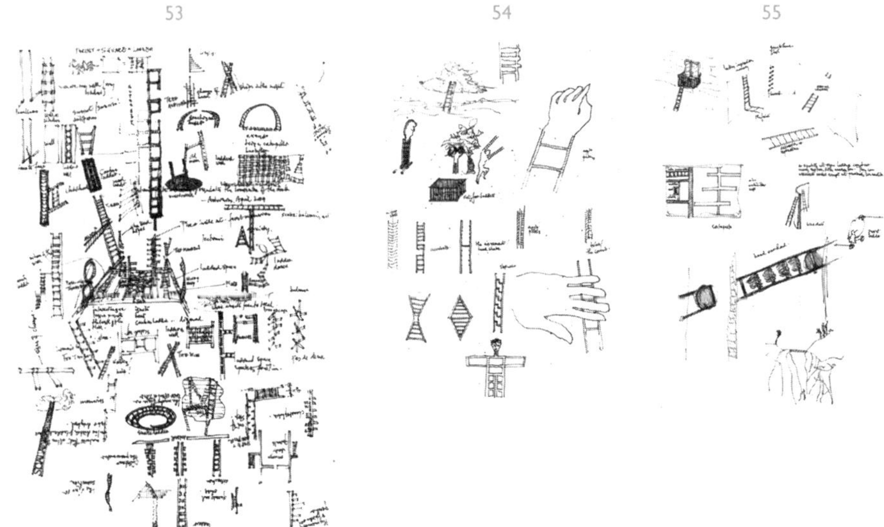

53   54   55

And a number of subsequent, also unrealized,
public art engagements - *Laddered* (Forrest Place,
Perth, May 2009, PLATE 19), *Ladder Awry*
(TarraWarra Museum of Art, August 2012, FIG 56),
Laddered Trellis (Union Street, Melbourne, 2016,
PLATE 18) – afforded opportunities to explore
the choreotopographical potential
of the ladder further.

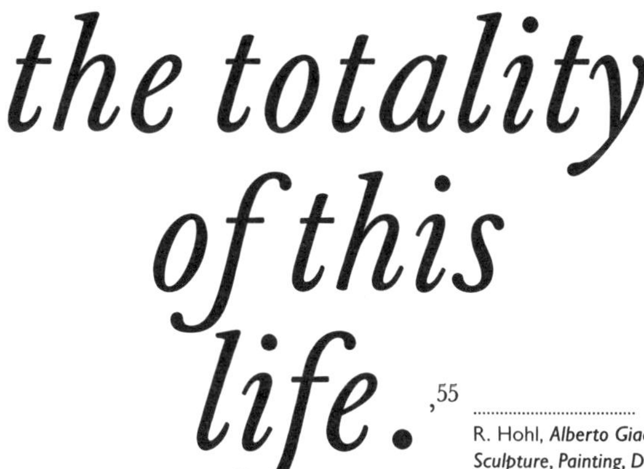

56

In these, the ladder, usually twisted like a dancer,
makes manifest a collective will: a gesture of Eros,
the Public Worker, it rehumanises or animates buildings
and spaces, relating the self-sufficient abstraction of their design to
the outside world Giacometti evoked when he wrote, 'Every moment
of the day people come together and drift apart, and approach each
other again to try to make contact anew. They unceasingly form and
reform living compositions of incredible complexity' and, Giacometti
added, 'What I want to express in everything I do, is

the totality of this life.,55

R. Hohl, *Alberto Giacometti:
Sculpture, Painting, Drawing,*
London: Thames and Hudson,
1972, 31.

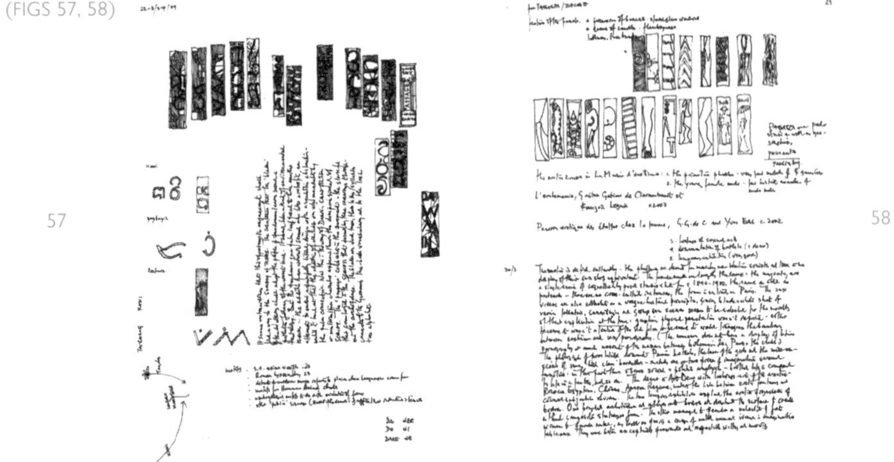

Sociable metamorphoses of the ladder in this spirit include
the stelae proposed for *Zipcode*, a wayfinding design in Darwin
(FIGS 57, 58)

and early sketches for *Pearl*, a cultural centre and
landscape at the Darwin Waterfront (FIG 59), both from mid 2009.

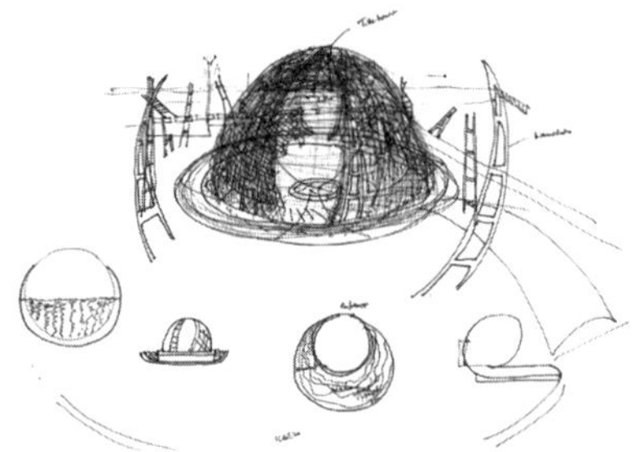

Pearl emerged as an accomplished
concept by Edmund Carter.
The stumbling proto-forms I explored,
concentric semicircles of walls, split
spheres and other volute variants,
had precedents in public art proposals
made as part of *Red Ways*, a place-making engagement in Alice
Springs. *Red Ways* was a drawn-out affair, in the end more useful
as a laboratory for the exploration of cross-cultural forms in the
context of making places after their stories than for any impact
on professional practice or regional governance.[56]

The operations wrought on the ladder motif,
for example,
did not produce a lasting result; they were, though,
an accurate graphic diary of the twists and turns
of the project itself
as we sought to reconcile cultural conflicts, administrative inertia
and professional self-interest.

The saga is told in Paul
Carter, *Places Made
After Their Stories:
design and the art of
choreotopography*, Perth:
UWAP, 2015,101-145.

Groups of sociable figures (FIGS 60-62) morphed
into studies of signage, street furniture and a new
kind of cowled form – a twisted or involuted
cylinder enclosing a ladder (FIG 63).

60

In another development,

the ladder was laid out on the ground and used
as a longitudinal grid running the length of
Todd Street between Wills Terrace and Sturt
Terrace. PLATE 20 incorporates memories
of the *Tracks* project, while its recessed forms
recall the Soane sarcophagus. I imagined the
grid as the cross-section of the energy field
running through the town's under surface.
A riff on the historical role Alice Springs played
as a repeater station in the early days of the
Overland Telegraph, the nodal points and
intervals discovered in this way were interpreted
as information about the place's rhythmic
geography – offering designers

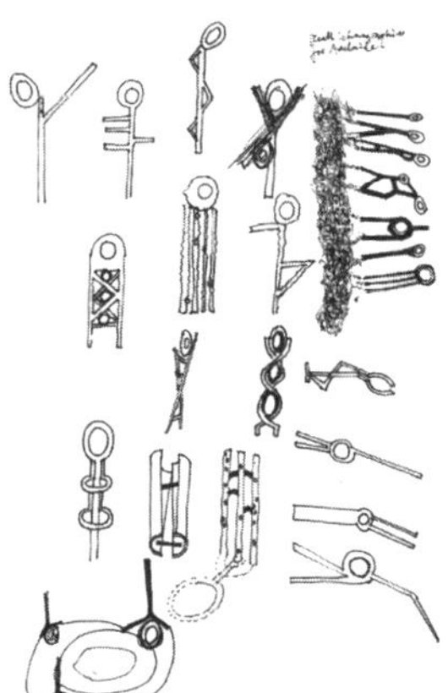

choreotopographical hints

(PLATES 21 and 22 , FIG 65)

•

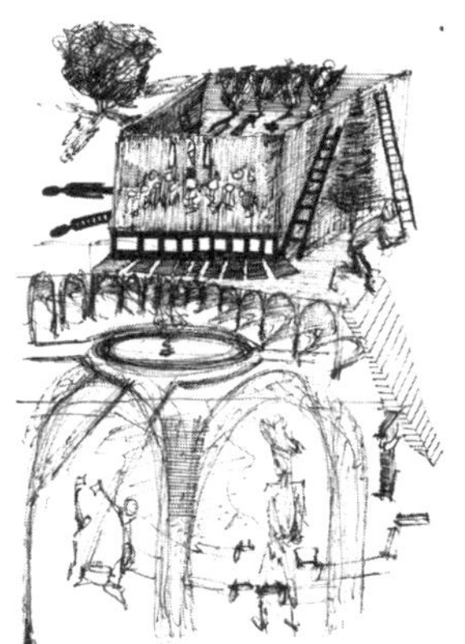

63

we imagined the location of sculptural elements in terms of environmental acupuncture, our way markers as

needles pushed into the
pressure points of the earth,
releasing blocked-up passages and re-animating
the seasonal flow paths of water,
above and below ground,
and the relationship of their routes to the root ſtocks
and tree lineages

grown up (FIG 64)

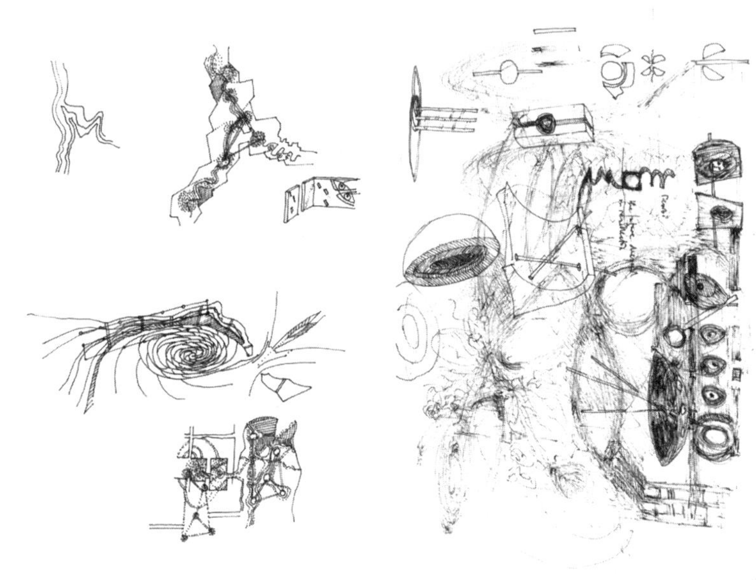

64

65

along those
ancestral
ways.

L A
T E
S

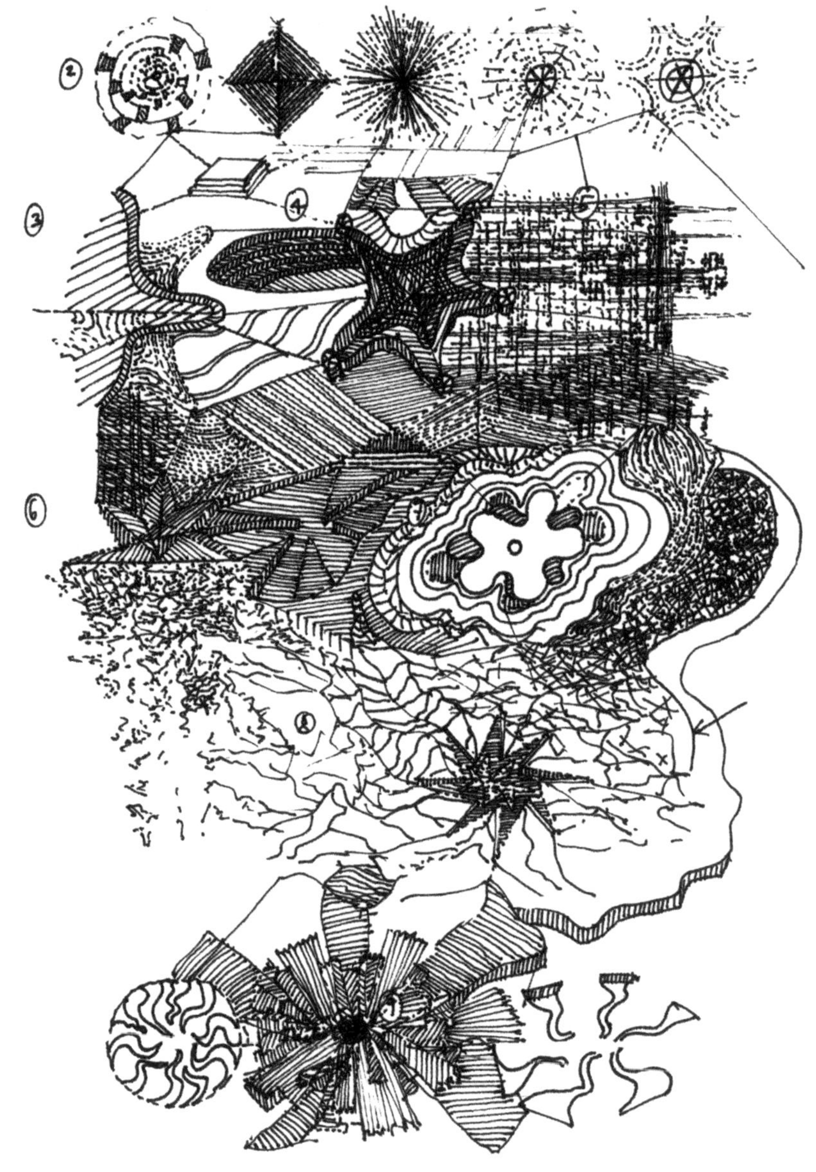

Plate 1

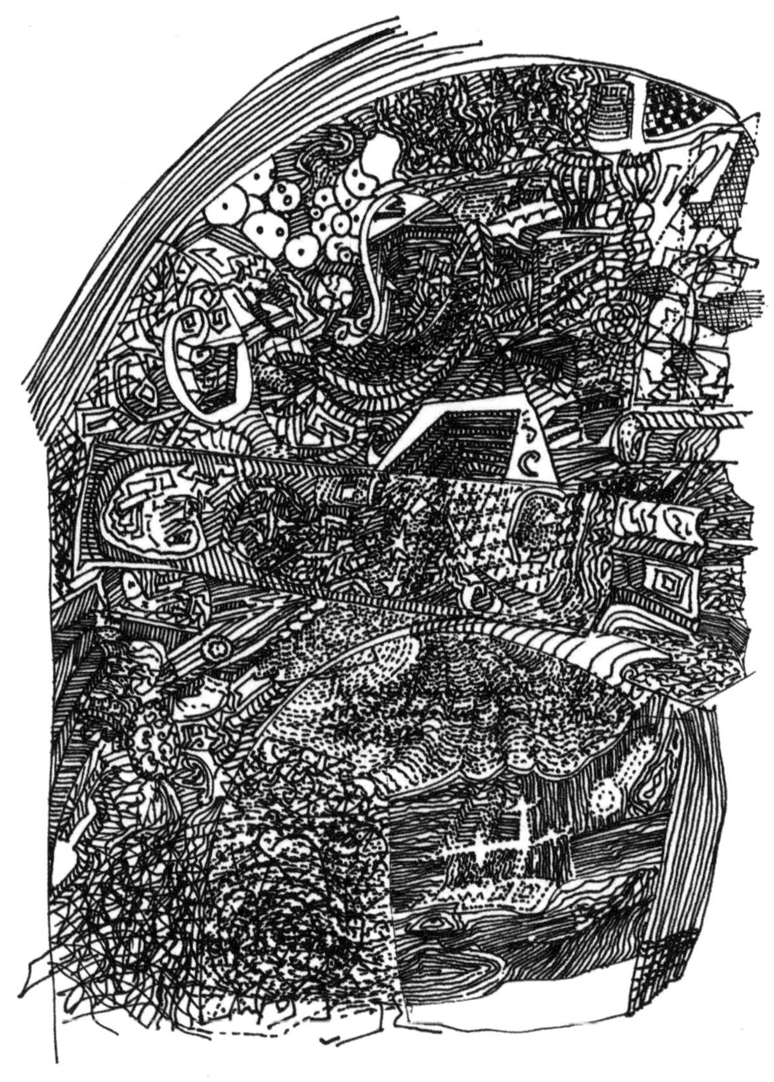

Plate 3

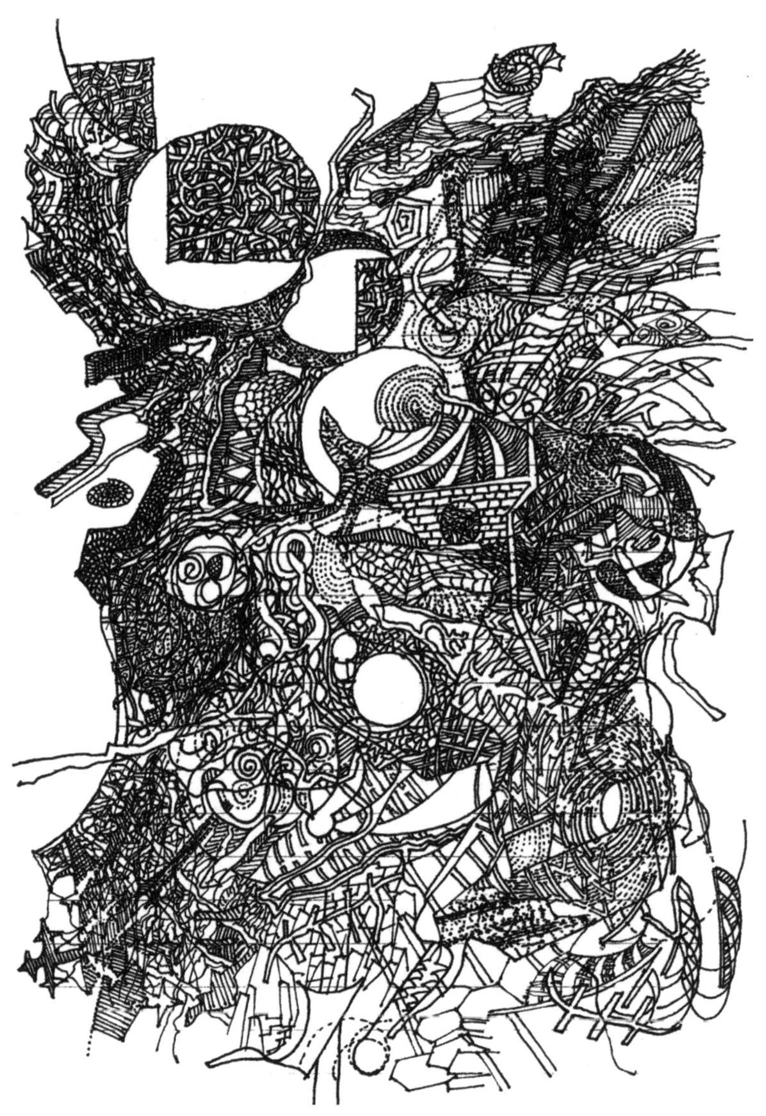

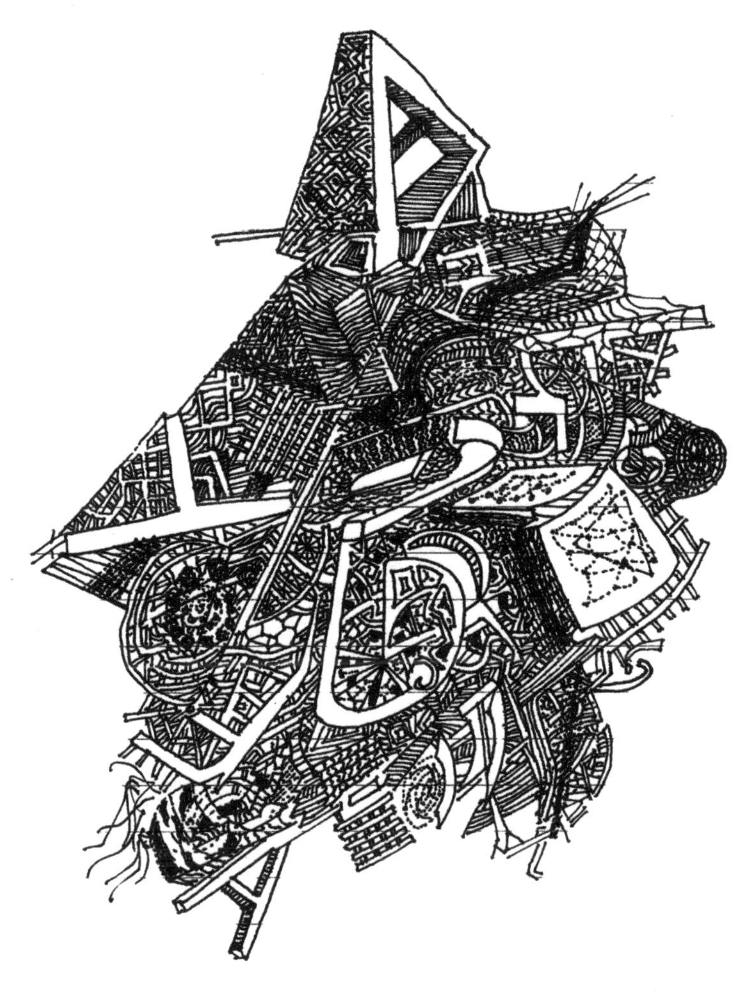

Plate 9

Plate 11

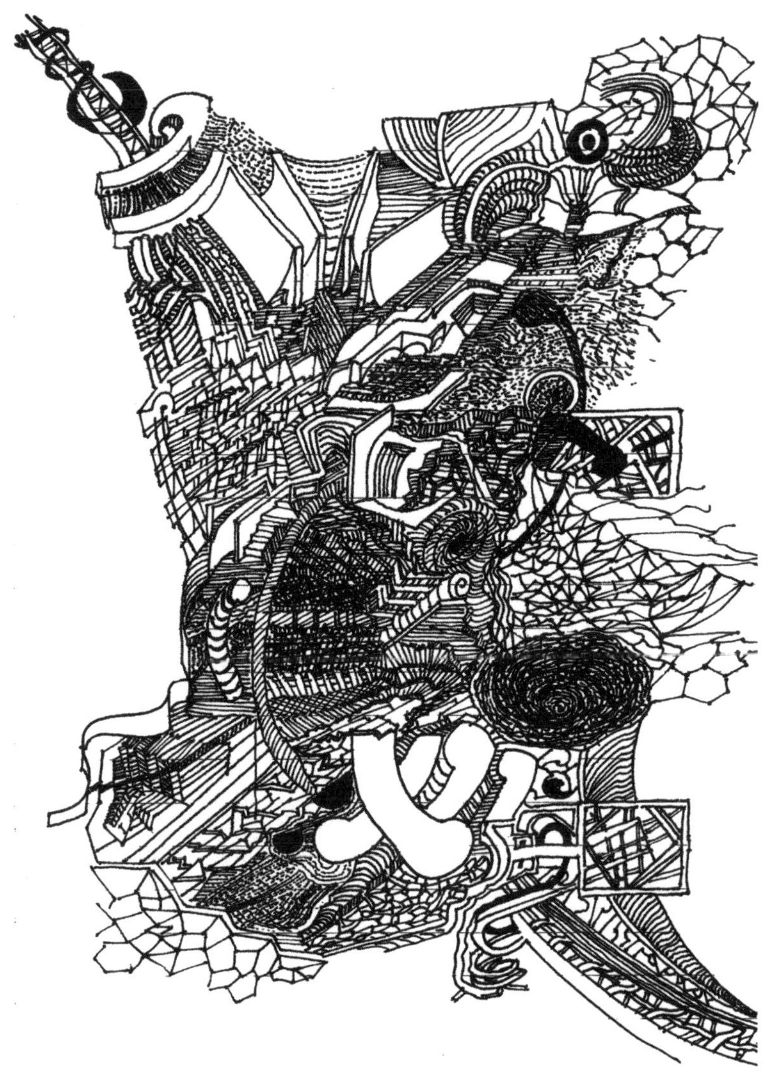

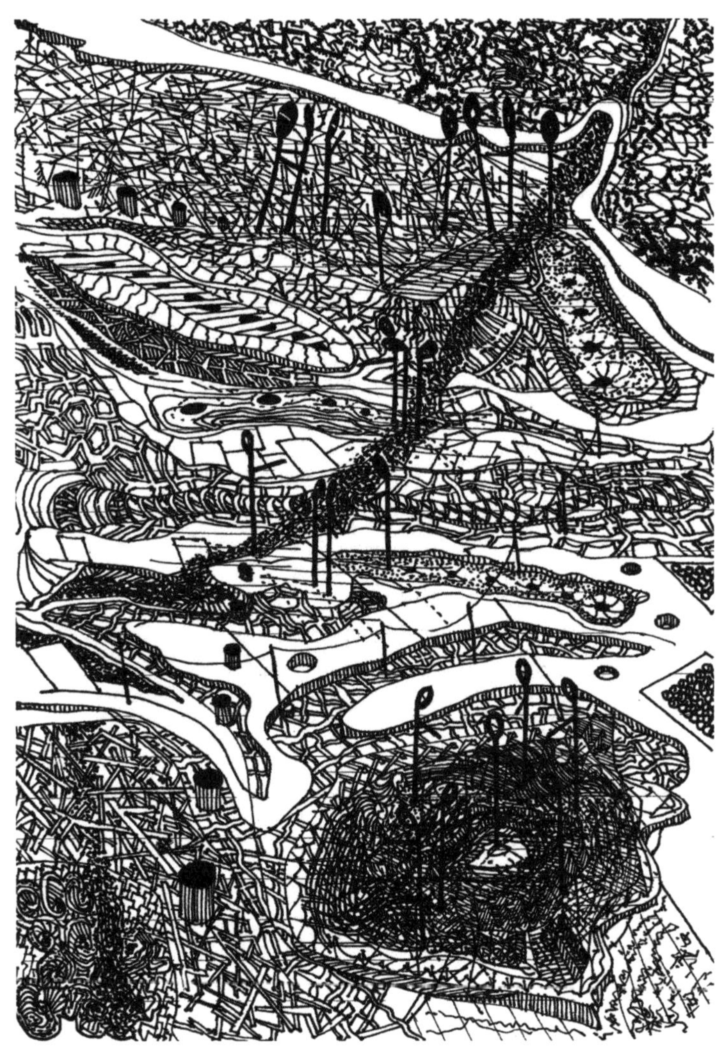

Plate 15

5/7

- inscriptions or programmes . the Motto
- heritage . celebration
- website template
- Peace flame
- reflect cultural . intellectual & environmental legacy   for 21st-Century Vision   G.G. - Pleiades.

- follow for masonline - cluster techniques.

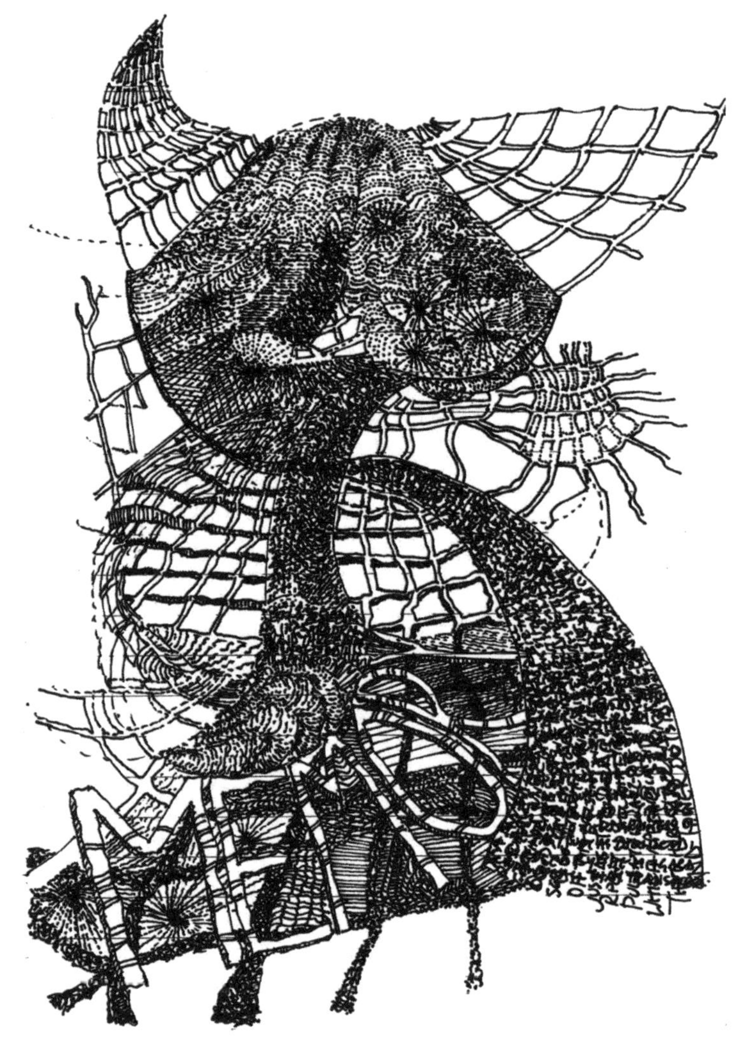

Plate 18

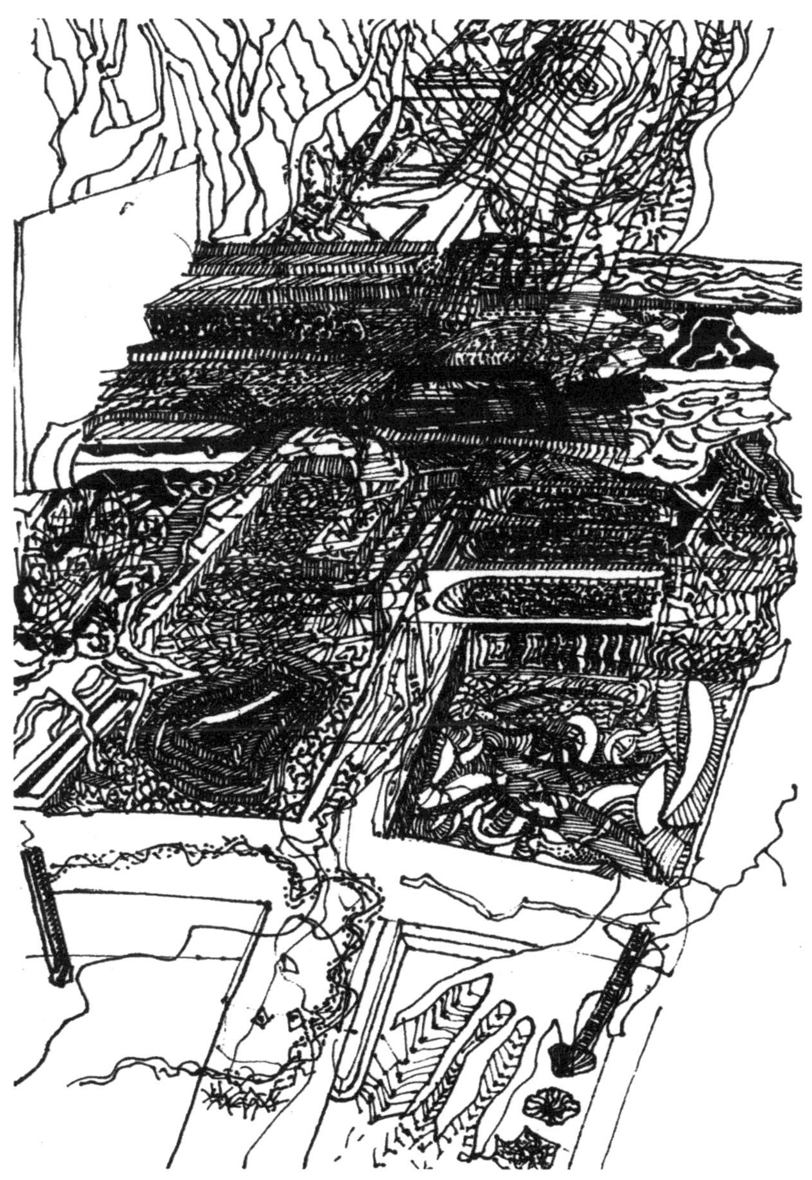

Plate 20

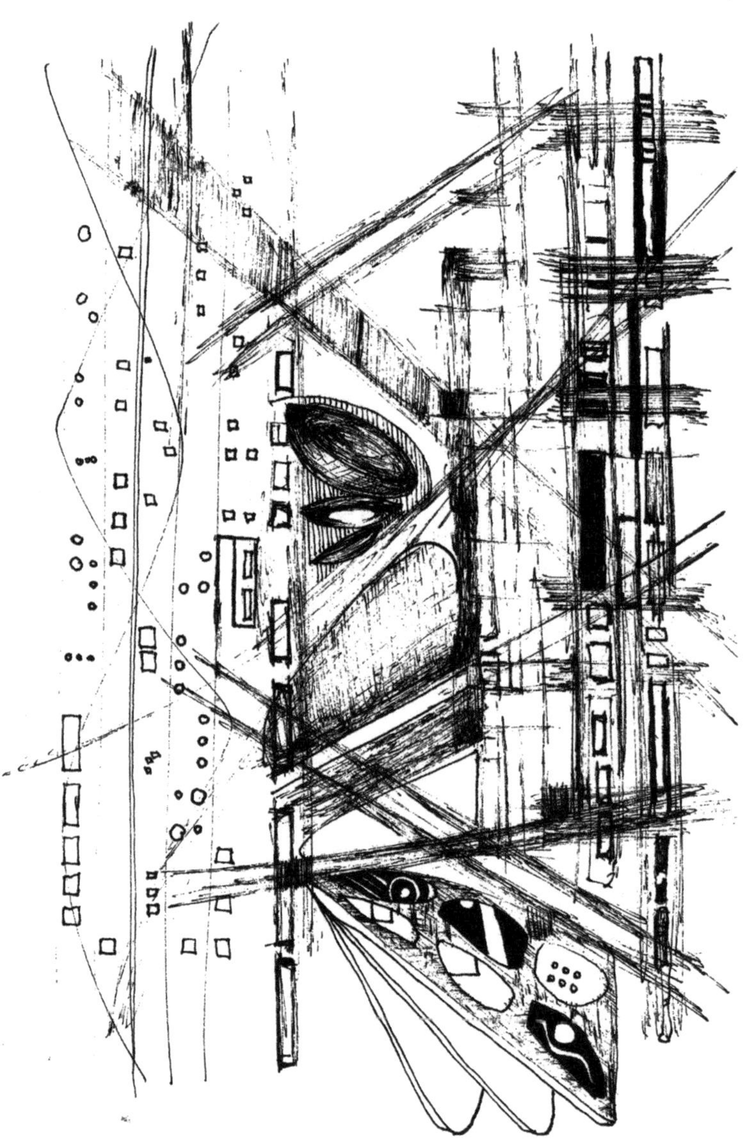

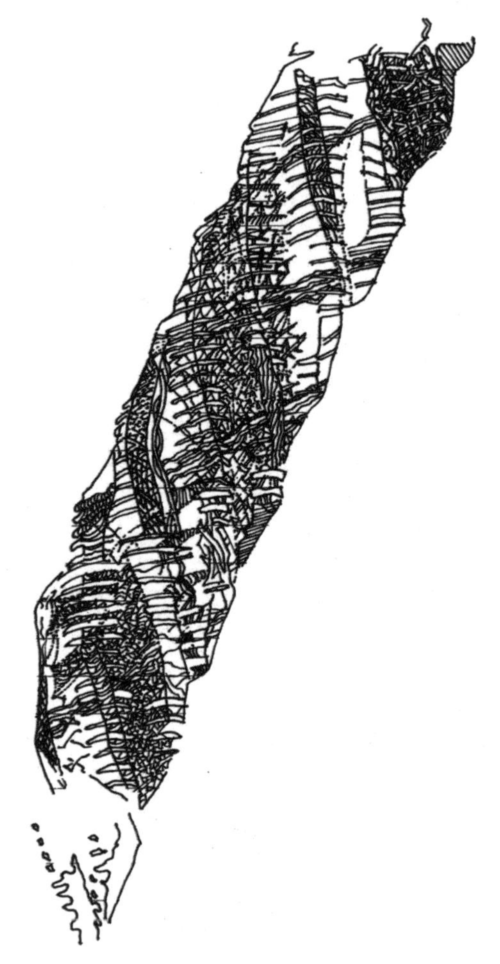

Plate 23

102

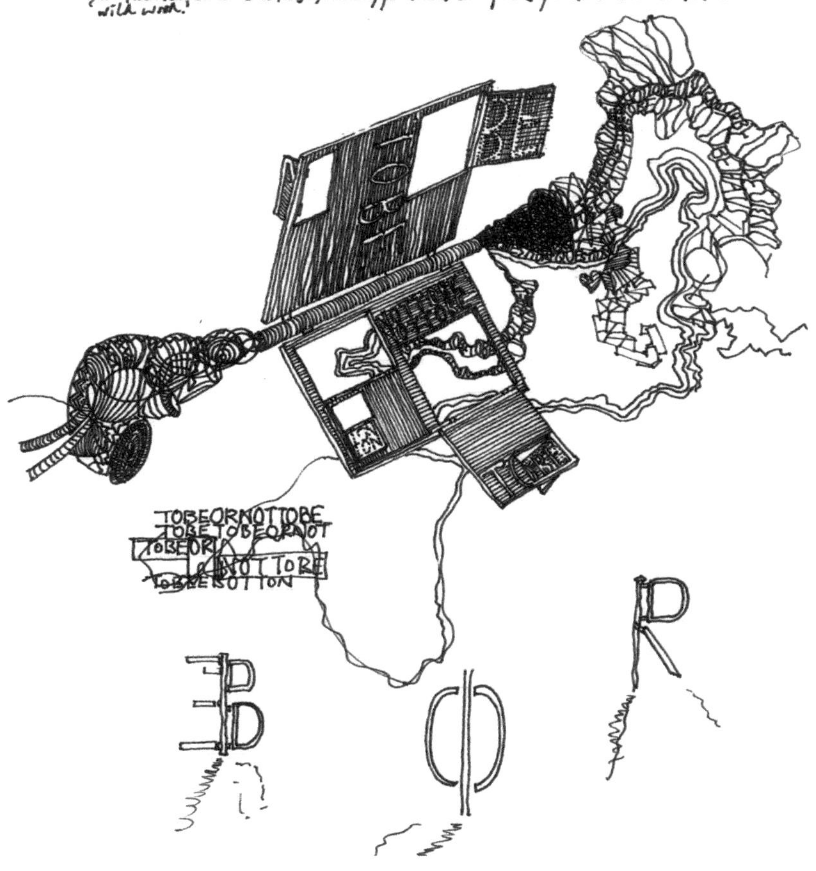

TOBEORNOTTOBE
TOBETOBEORNOT
TOBEOR NOTTOBE
TOBERSOTTON

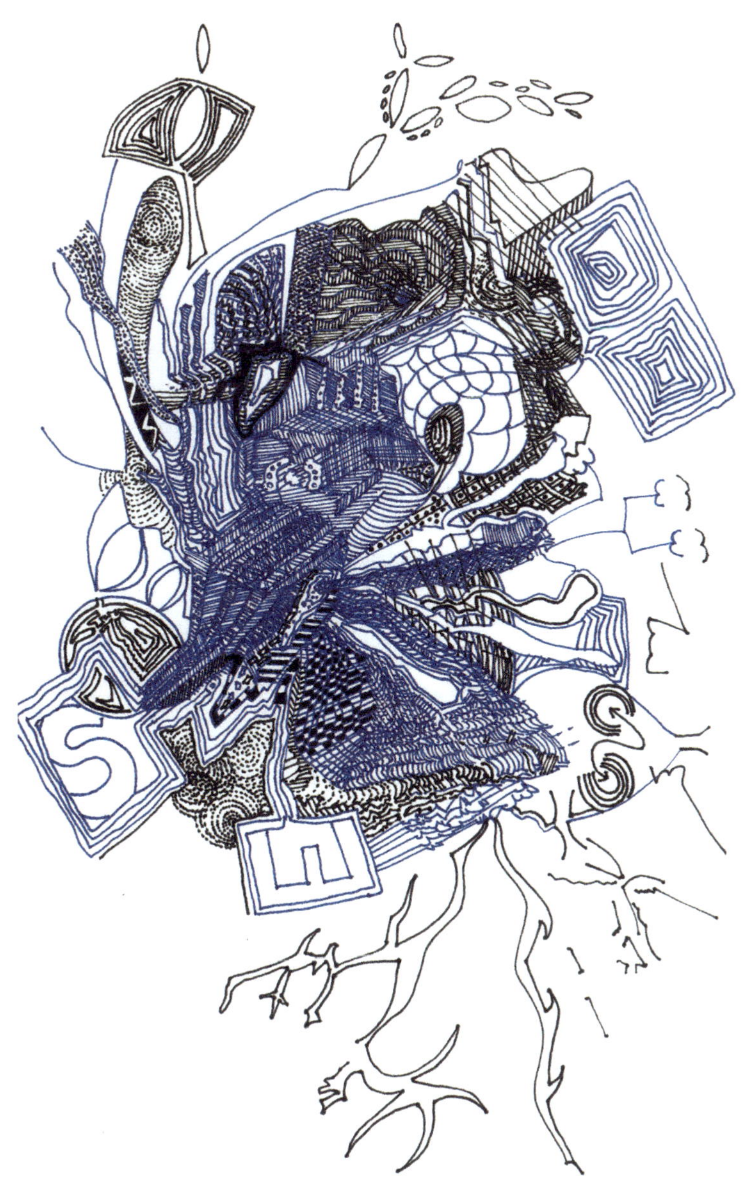

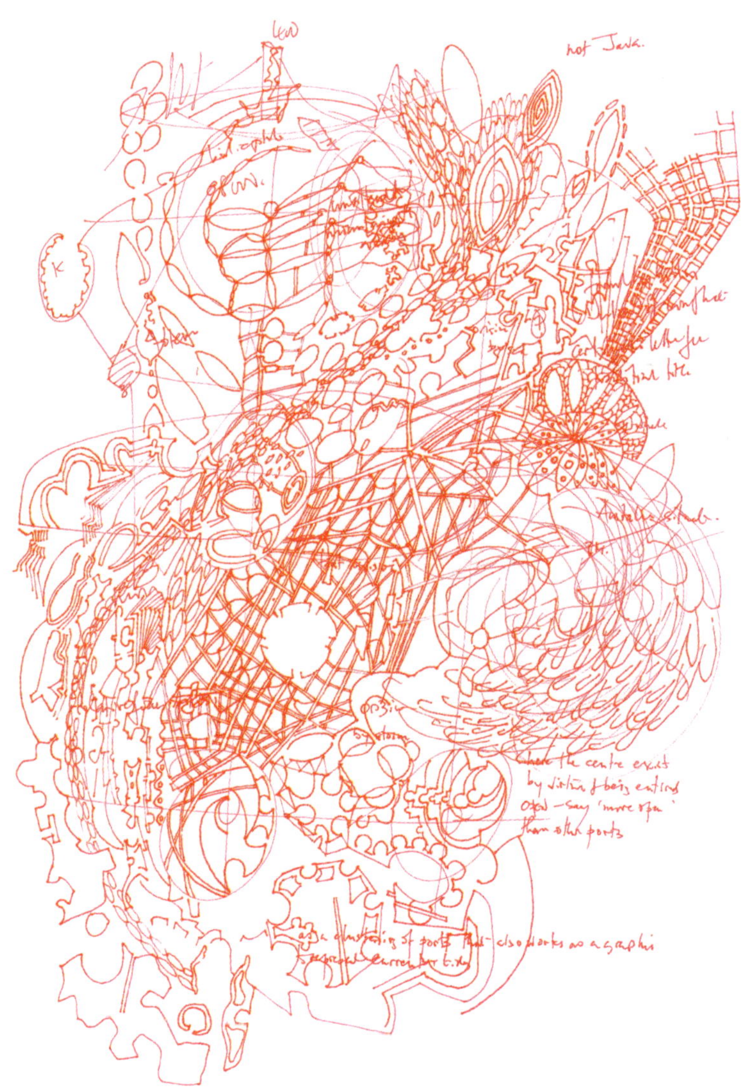
hot Java.

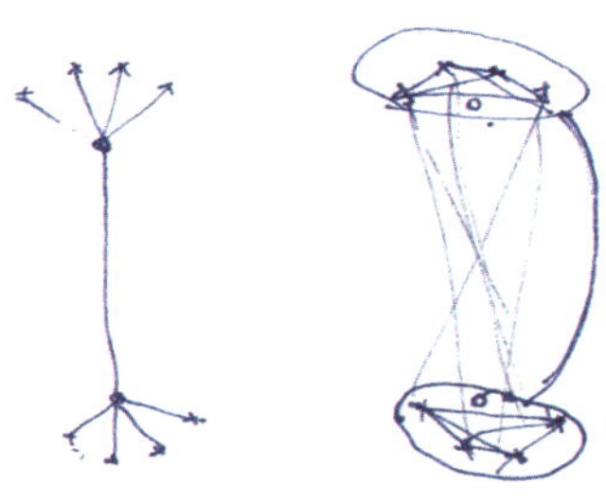

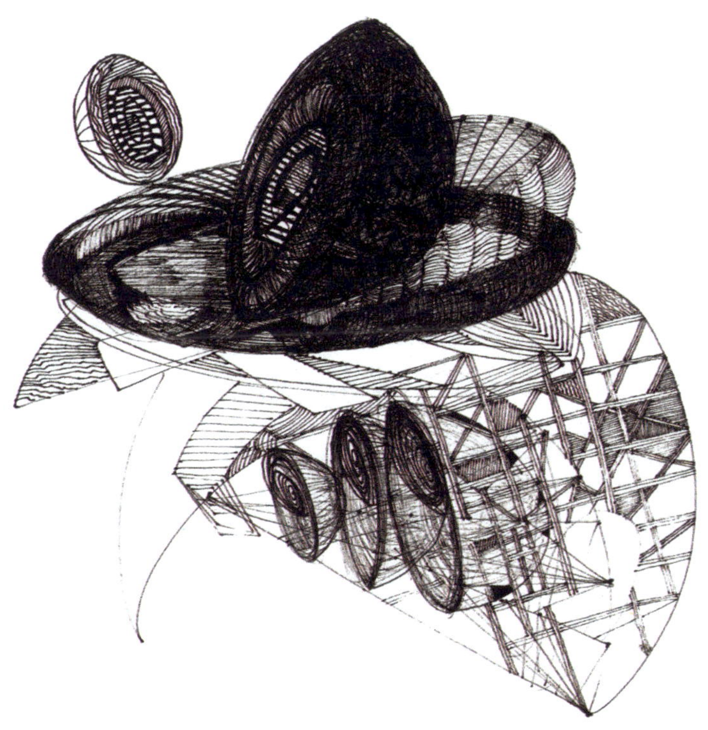

Connect to this

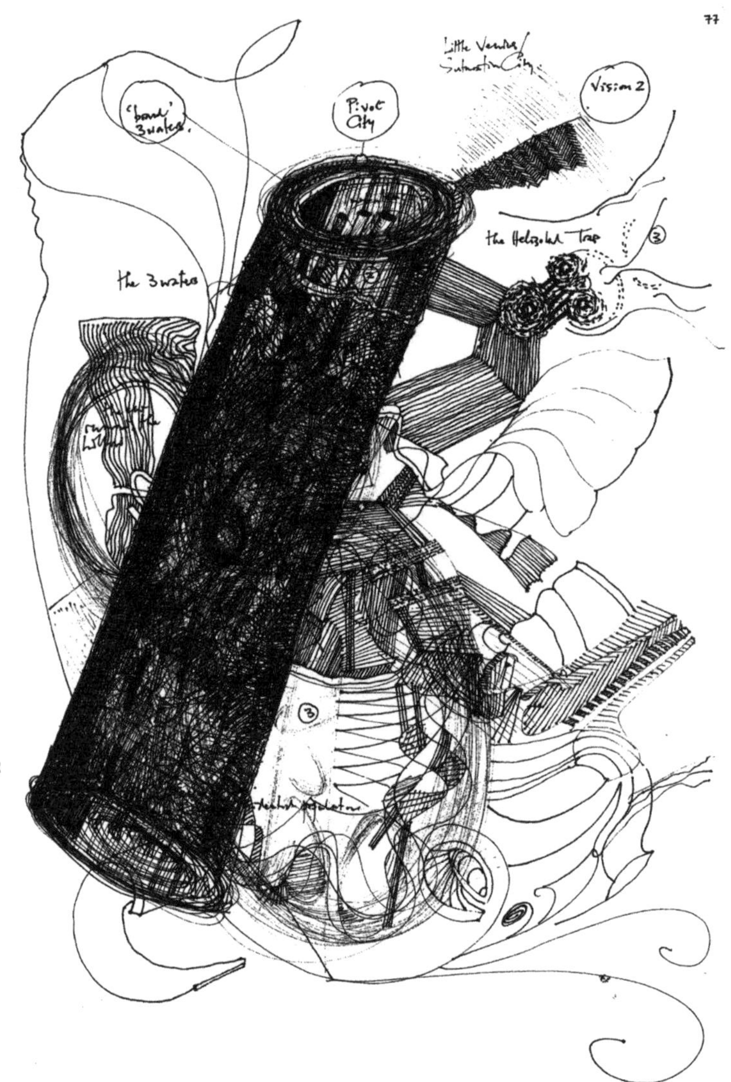
'bowl'
3 waters
Pivot
City
Little Vanbru /
Submarine City
Vision 2
the Helipdal Trap
the 3 waters
3

BACKGROUND
PROJECT
STORIES
INFORMATION

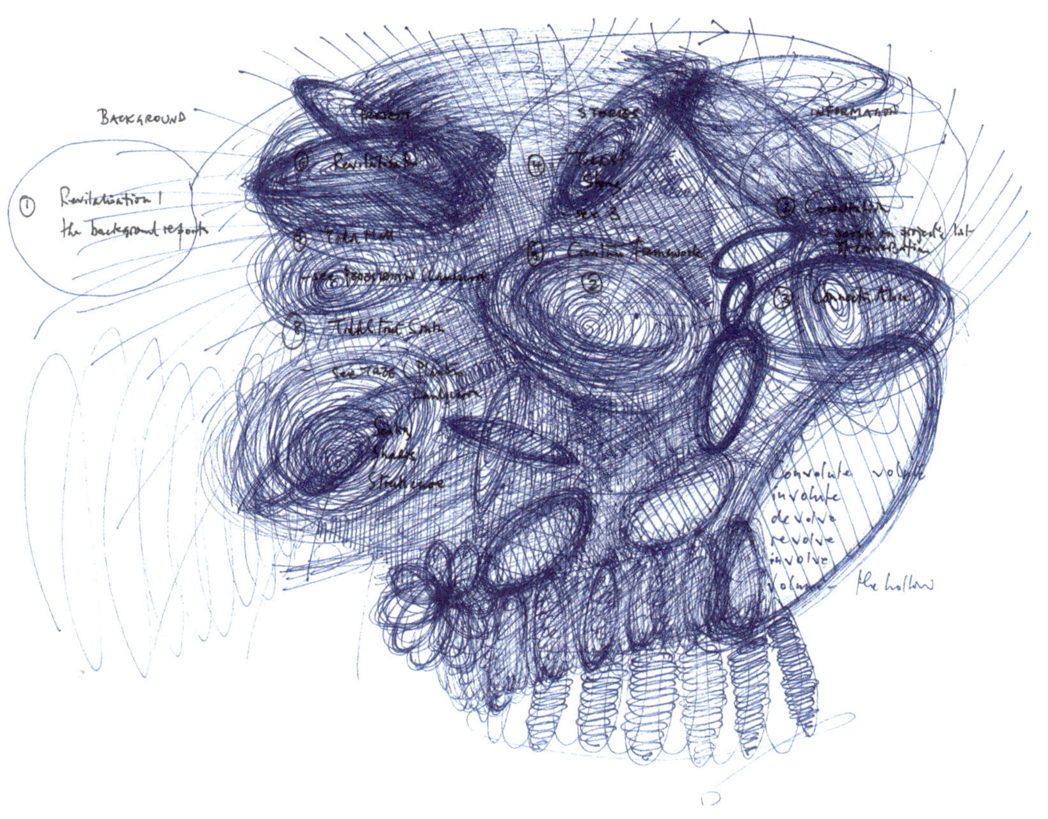

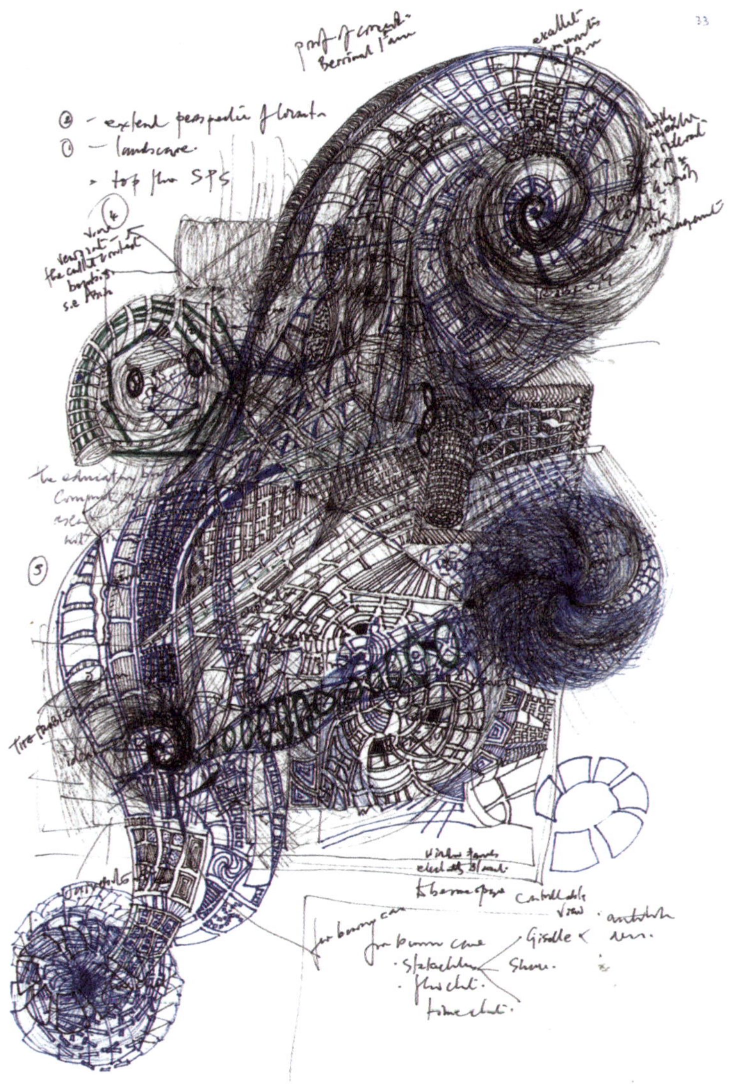

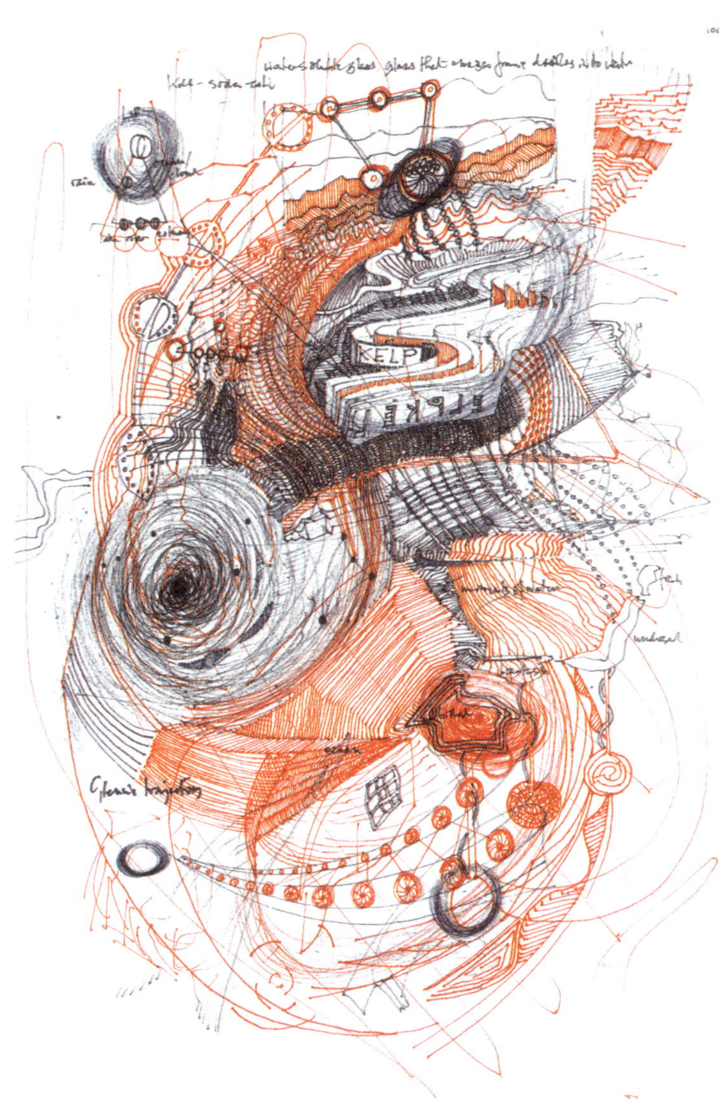

Plate 32

Plate 33

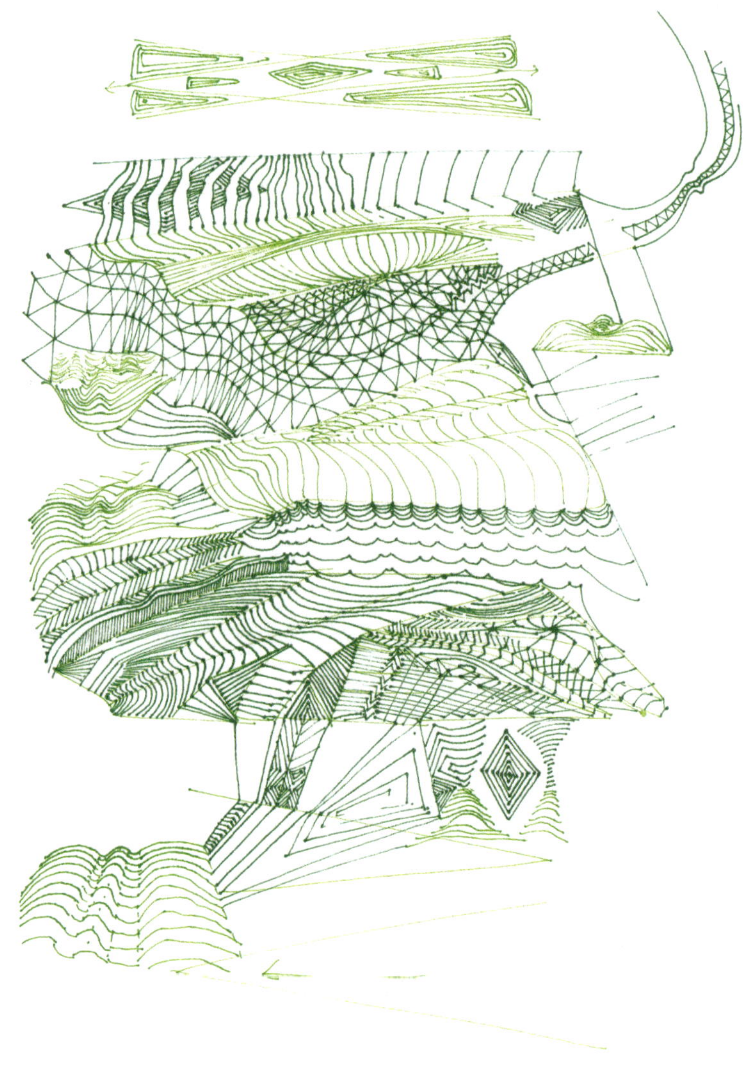

Plate 35

114

Plate 36

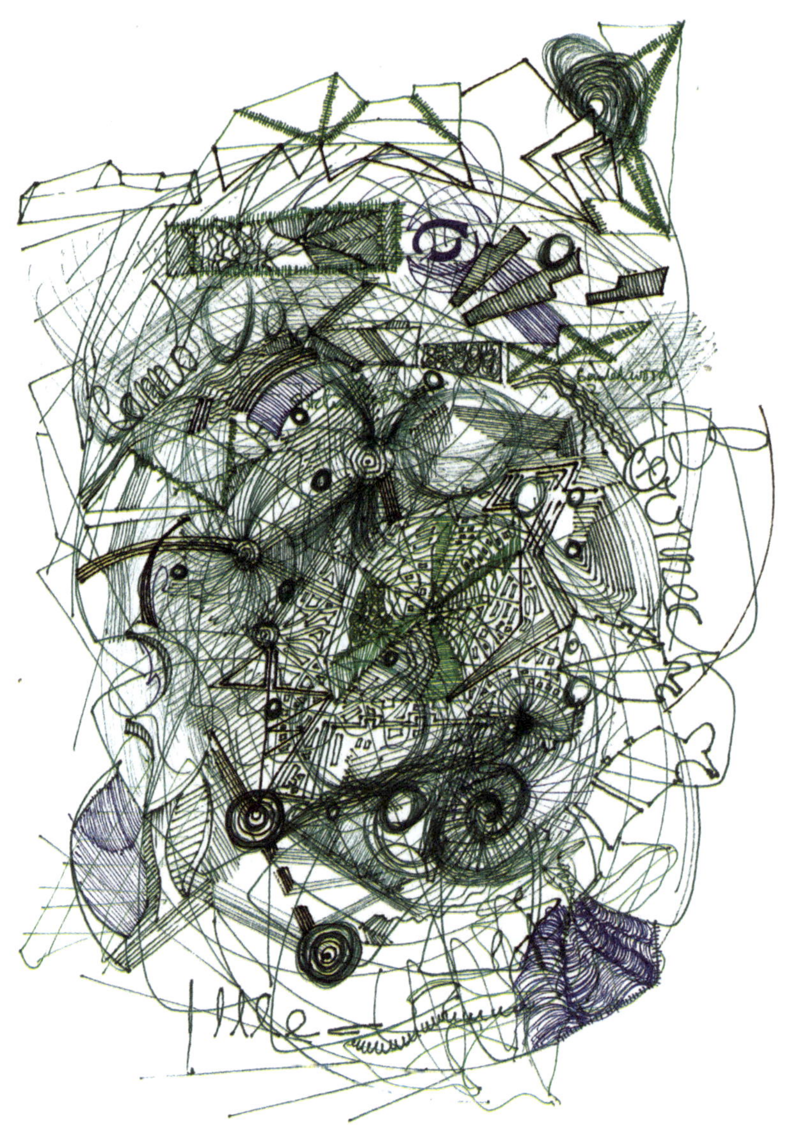

Plate 37

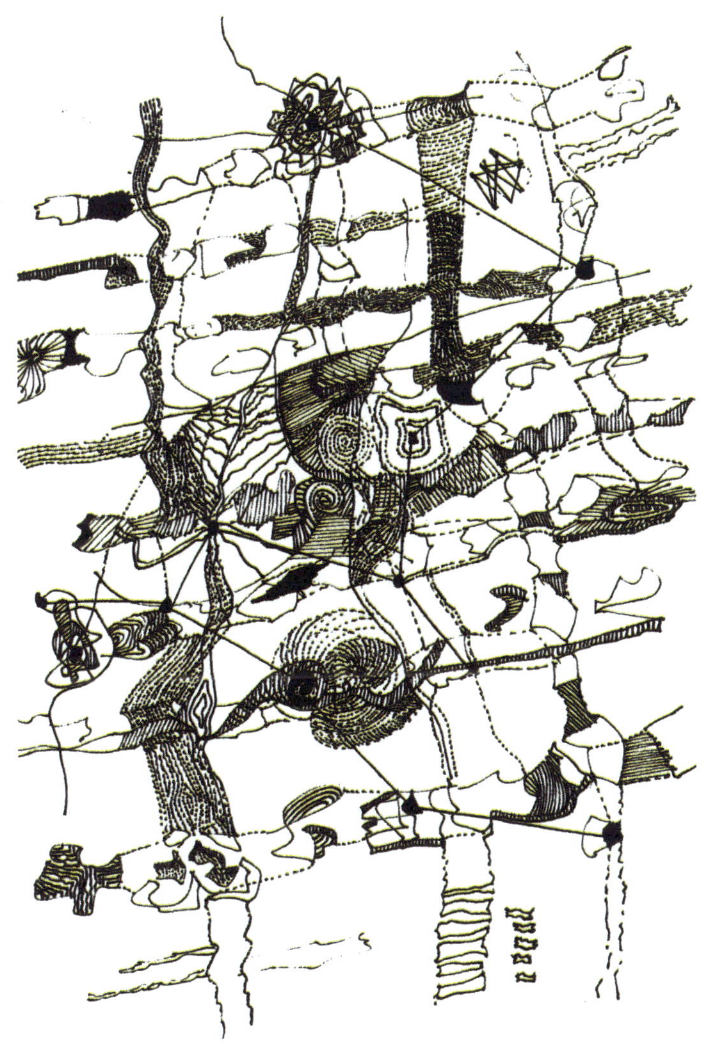

Plate 39

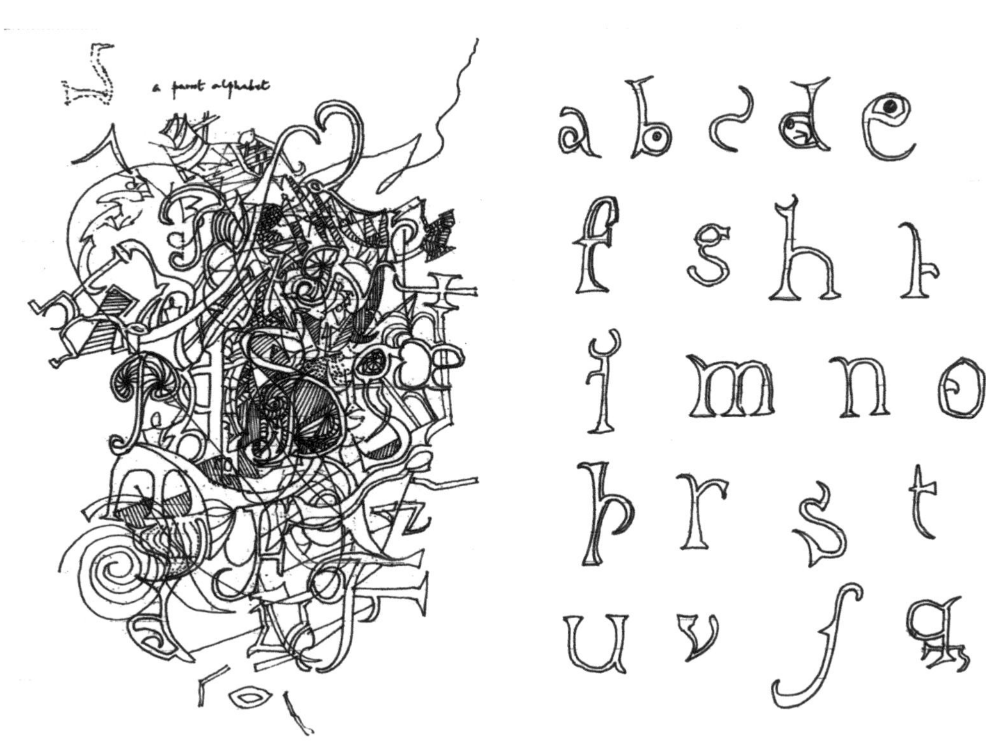

a facet alphabet

Plate 43

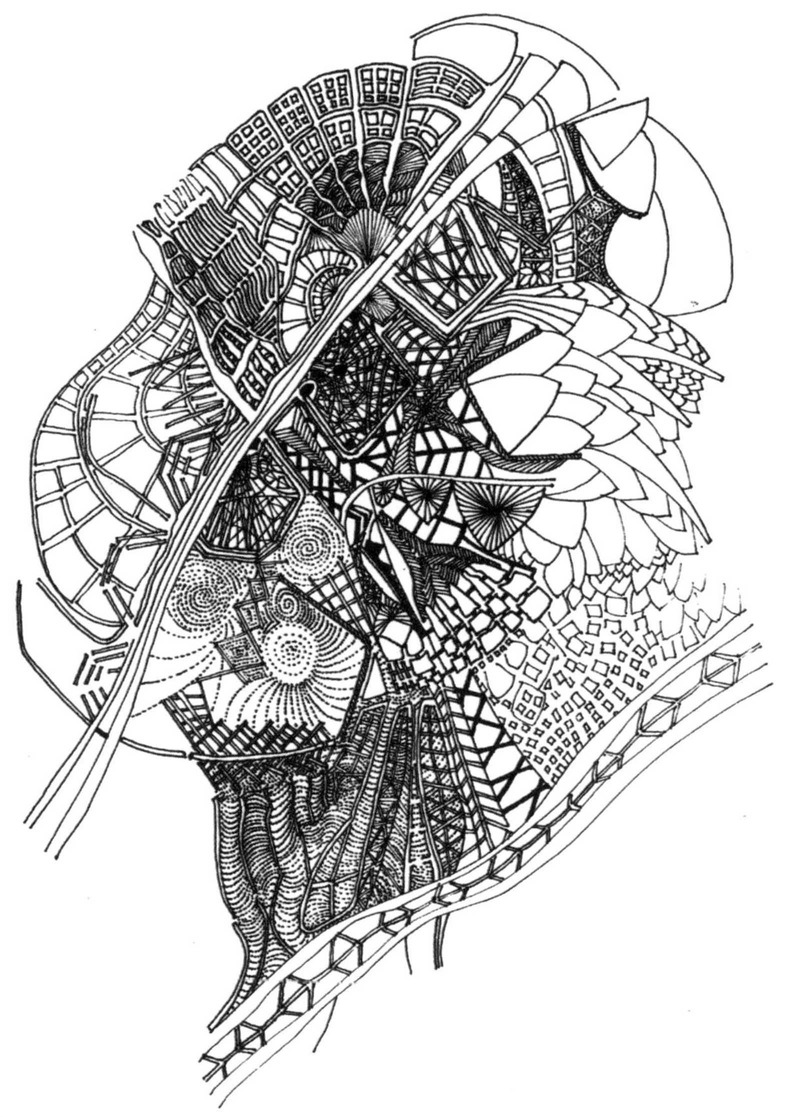

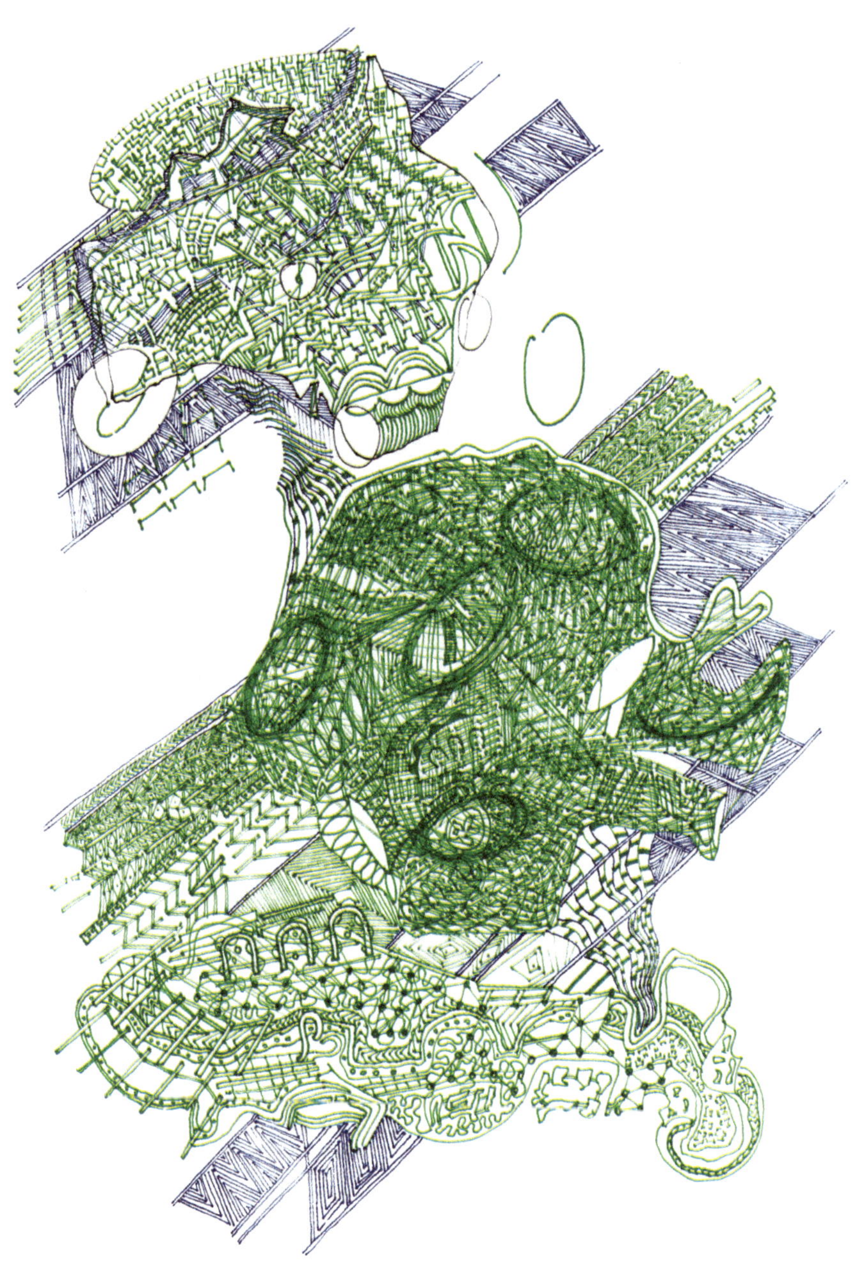

Plate 45

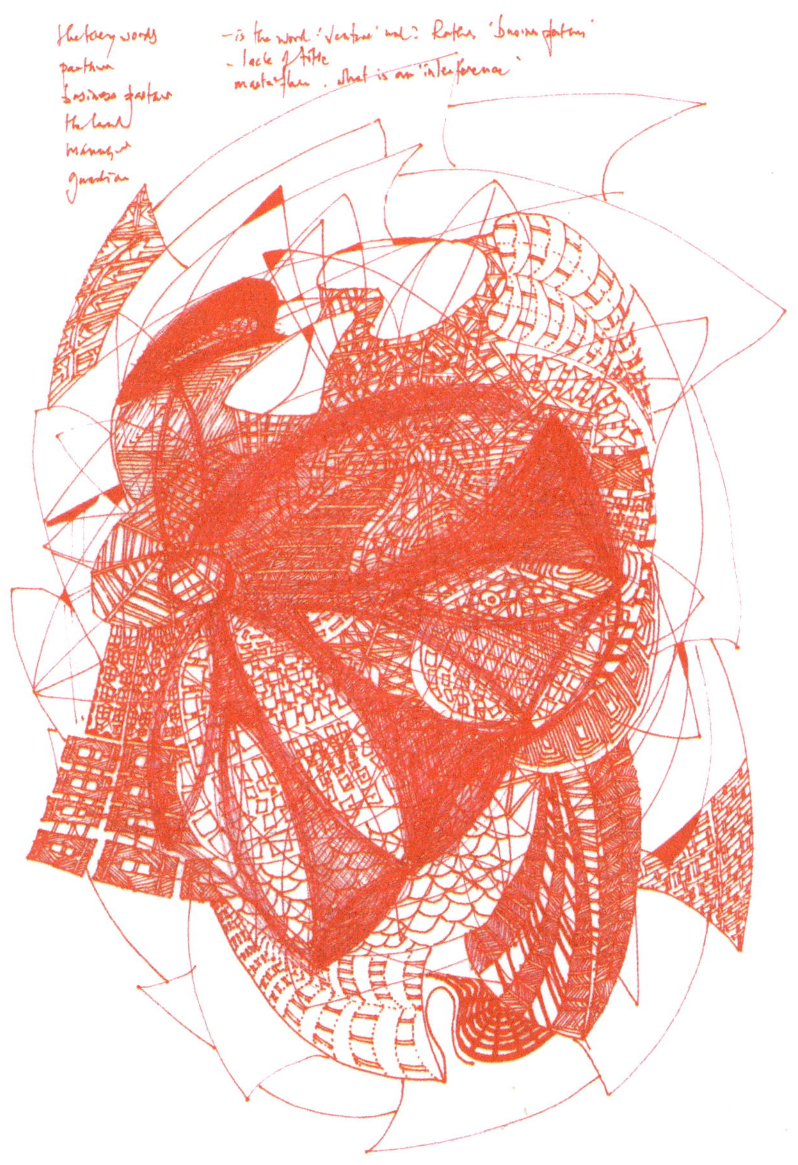

the key words
partner
business partner
the land
manager
guardian
—is the word 'venture' not? Rather 'business partner'
- lack of title
masterplan . what is an 'interference'

Plate 46

6.

Writing this commentary,

I am surprised to find how many of the doodles,

cartoons, sketches or other thought forms inform or seed public art, landscape design and even master planning projects in which I participated. Some of these 'real world' exercises have been published, and readers could be forgiven for wondering whether *Neglected Dimensions* repeats what has already been written elsewhere. However, this is not true. The derivations of projects described in such publications as *Dark Writing* and *Places Made After Their Stories* are presented as the materialization of poetic philosophies: little or nothing is said about their graphic conceptualization, or about the role even vestigial sketches play in exploring the compositional intelligence of gesture,

or the place-making value of movement forms.

This suggests a deep-rooted schism in intellectual culture and its academic reflection. Hypothesis-forming and problem-solving are common to all domains of knowledge; however, the translation between diegetic and diagrammatic research is attenuated in the extreme[57] –

Diegetic logic is narrative-based, defined in terms of the fulfilment, or annulment, of certain forming premises. Diagrammatic logic is non-narrative and depends on the immediate recognition factor in the design of a plausible composition.

as the sharp division in scholarly publishing programs, between cultural theory, on the one hand, and art and design practice, on the other, illustrates. In fact, as emerges here, the ease with which writing drifts into drawing, and drawing serves to draw out an idea, suggest a reintegrated practice of shaping, simultaneously conceptual and compositional.

Wordcoils had been a feature of the early thoughts about Federation Square. Over the next few years, they assumed increasingly complex volumetric articulation (FIGS 66- 68). They took on a new lease of life in *Hamlet's Mill*, a public art and education project proposed for the River Thames, designed to raise awareness about climate change and its representation. The central trope, or mythopoetic provocation, was the identification of Shakespeare's Hamlet with the Norse hero, Amlethi who, when the original axle tree of the world was kicked out of true - an event marked by the inception of the maelstrom of change - was charged with managing the new turbulence.[58]

Giorgio de Santillana & Hertha von Dechend, *Hamlet's Mill: an essay investigating the origins of human knowledge and its transmission through myth*, Boston: David R. Godine, 1969, 87-95.

The challenge for our new old Amlethi/Hamlet, here representing London's traditional embrace of complex societal and political change, was to become or not to become - a rhetorical choice as anthropogenically-induced environmental transformation leaves us no choice but to adapt.

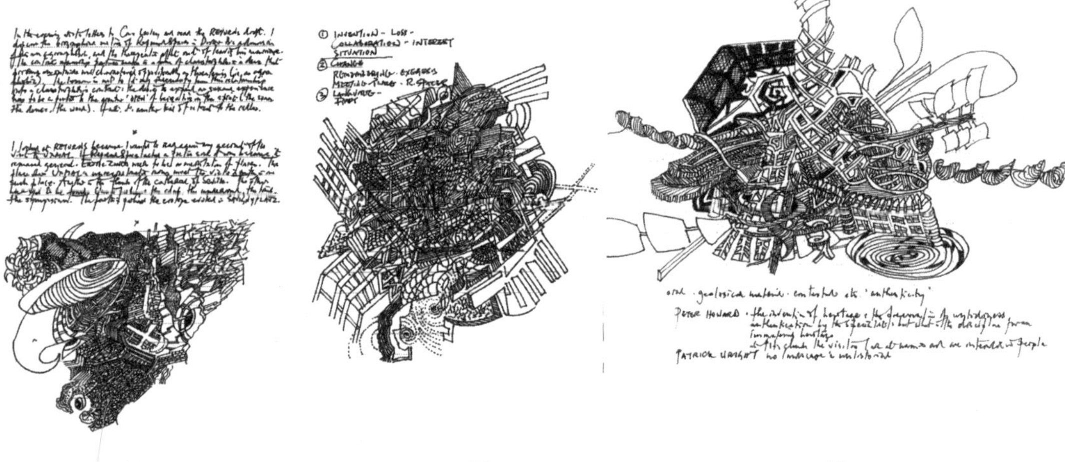

66

67

68

The focus of *Hamlet's Mill* was on the ethics and aesthetics of climate change data selection and presentation: to what extent do alarming future scenarios misrepresent the turbulence of change, and how may more complex, nuanced transmissions equip us to conceptualise our situation better? The armature for embedding the mathematics of complexity in the information display itself – the new Hamlet's Mill - was imagined as a turbine (FIG 69). We took local inspiration from the fact that the Tate Modern incorporated a former Turbine Hall, and from other local icons of revolution, including Shakespeare's Globe Theatre.

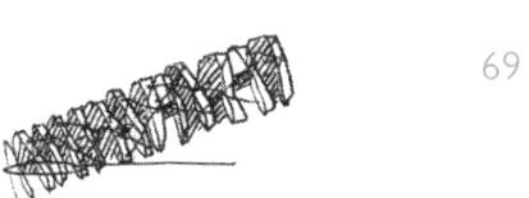

In one version *Hamlet's Mill* displayed information derived from climate monitoring stations as a wordcoil spun through the Tate Turbine Hall (FIG 70, PLATE 23). I noted, 'Hydrologists tell us that turbulence in water stabilises when a double vortex forms. Two spirals spin round each other, creating at their centre a tube or spindle. *Hamlet's Mill* is a double spiral that is stable, although constantly changing. It is being as becoming.'[59]

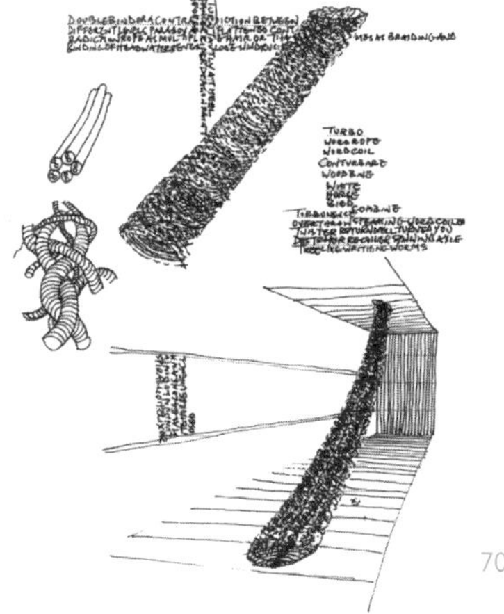

The emergence of the double spiral as a stabilizing structure within turbulent systems models a physical mechanism analogous to Parmenides's 'gate filled with gates' located at the transition between Night and Day, as described in his poem *The Way of Truth*. It is a structure always open to change but itself changeless (PLATE 24).

Paul Carter, '"Maelstrom" and the *informe* of information', lecture, School of Architecture, University of Newcastle, UK, June 23, 2008, 1-32, 13. Unpublished.

Such a device goes on changing:

if there were no measurable change in the universe, it would have no reason for being. Yet its being

stands out against the flux
as a constant
presence.

To possess these seemingly contradictory qualities is the genius of the double spiral, which also produces its own 'tube' or 'spindle'. Generating the spindle, it can be thought of as a multiplication of gates:
the gates are not 'within' the door, but are the fluctuating shields or louvres that scintillate up and down the curving ramps as they turn

on their own axis.

In this case, the spiral arms can be programmed to scintillate in non-linear, non-progressive ways. The pattern does not progress towards some goal (crisis, flooding, irremediable change) but is a constant fluctuation, like the scintillations caused by sub-atomic particles as they

flash up inside the vacuum tube.

The construction of the spiral arms remained vague but the line they were to describe was clear.

It is not a single, directionally-consistent line that represents a cumulative change in the environment (rising average sea levels, rising average temperatures, or a combination of these) – instead, the closest analogue is the arabesque. The arabesque is the line of errancy, representing change as an aimless process governed by nothing beyond the will of the wanderer. Its best literary exemplar, I noted, was Thomas De Quincey, in whose writing a consistent effort is made to derive the form of the work from the 'involutes' of self-consciousness. 'De Quincey describes the data of consciousness without regard for Newtonian conventions of time and space: the remotest past and the most immediate present are joined by association and mingle in the act of mediate reasoning. The pattern of associations that develops in this way is not defined by an external boundary and has no consistent direction. It can be likened to the experience of a city when it is walked without any business whatsoever. It can also be likened to the flow of water when it is studied for the eddies that constitute its turbulent texture, rather than for the course carved out by its banks.'[60]

Carter, '"Maelstrom" and the *informe* of information', 28.

The *type* of this wayward devolution of the divine,
destructive and
sublime, was,
I suggested, the maelstrom. The physical form of *Hamlet's Mill* would
be the arabesque drawn out of the maelstrom: 'It may be no accident
that the physical form of the work is unclear, for the historical
reference of the work is not exactly to a machine (a mill,
a gate,
a pivot, or even
a May Pole or other vortical structure) but to *monitors* of turbulence,
whose feedback relationship to the phenomena in question has
to navigate between control and chaos (in its negative sense).'[61]
Drawings like PLATE 12 (a chiasmatic force field), PLATE 14
(an animated spindle) and PLATE 16 (a revolving axle) explore this
theme. The same drawings include a variety of vortical forms as well
as scale- or sail-like forms that could be related to
turbine vanes.

The period of the negotiations to make the *Hamlet's Mill*
project overlapped with three Australian design engagements:
Red Ways, Alice Springs,
Turning Point (later *Pearl*), Darwin and
Golden Grove, Sydney.

The impact of the turbulence studies on these
projects is obvious. PLATE 20 is a diagram
of a passage or traverse of the Alice Springs
town grid. It is conceived as a sequence of
eddies, and in some respects suggests that one
of the *Hamlet's Mill* sketches has been rifled,
key bits removed and laid out on the ground.
On the page preceding PLATE 15 is a sketch
for *Golden Grove*. It visualizes the constellation
of the Pleiades,

or Seven Sisters, as seven types of
maelstrom.

The implications of this project for publicly-funded research – and therefore public education – are discussed in Paul Carter, *Turbulence: climate change and the design of complexity*, Sydney: Puncher & Wattman, 2015, 53-64.

An earlier *Golden Grove* drawing PLATE 10 clearly
incorporates turbine blades, not to mention turbinate
shells, as well as older motifs
including erosion landscapes and faceted
terraces. In its recombination of motifs drawn
from diverse sources – motifs, further, that only
exist in combination – it illustrates graphically
De Quincey's already quoted proposition

that in memory
'perplexed combinations of *concrete*
objects, pass to us as *involutes* ...
in compound experiences incapable
of being disentangled.'

A third graphic improvisation for *Pearl* PLATE 28 also deploys
a now familiar range of motifs: lattices,
rigging,
ladders and
other coffered surfaces abound, but also spiraling arabesques,
involuted cross-sections and
revolving cones.

PLATES 25, 26 and 27 are related: lozenge motifs and open figures allude
to the cartographics of the famous atlas produced in Portugal around
1519 by Lopo Homem and Pedro Reinel, and now known as the *Miller
Atlas*. *Pearl* was in development at the same time as *Zipcode*, a public
artwork designed for State Square, Darwin. Celebrating the
proposition that Darwin was the gateway to south-east Asia,
Zipcode incorporated into the ground plane the
distinctive representation of islands as
concatenations of
openings.

Islands were groupings of
synapses, regions of intensified
flow and exchange. In the
archipelago – as in the possum cloak
patchwork – there are, strictly speaking,
no islands, as membership of the
group depends on being open to
change. The same can be said of
the ideation process informing
the emergence of distinct designs:
it sails here and there between
forming situations,
and any landfall in a definite project is
at best a landing place, behind and
flowing through what is built
is always the larger sea of fluctuating movement

forms here and there
contracting
into stable figures.

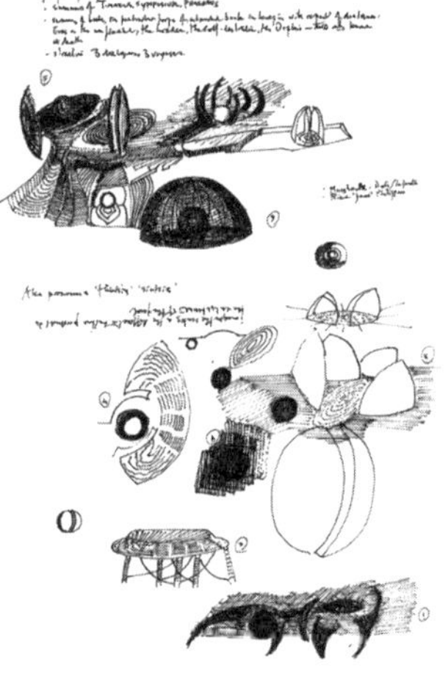

The projects mentioned here unfolded over periods
of years. They underwent numerous changes of
scope, different phases of community and
government interest and fluctuating client
commitment. They also overlapped one another:
some of the three dimensional formalisations of
the whirlpool metamorphose into helically-formed
hemispheres that appear as entrance markers in the
Alice Springs *Red Ways* project (FIG 71) and also
inform the structures sketched for *Pearl*
in Darwin (FIGS 72, 73).

71

72

73

I mentioned the uptake of these notebook sketches – and their
transformation into the language of CAD, but their freedom, and
their apparent lack of utility, is also important.
It maps
a between-projects region of ideation,
a reflective realm of speculation that can be compared to
the inner monologue that often shadows outer conversation. For they
are
discursive notations in the sense that they anticipate dialogue:
instances of 'drawing out aloud,' they chart an idealized
collaboration between manual intelligence,
eidetic fantasy and human situation.

A doodle like FIG 68 represents nothing so much as
a crossing place,
a composite arabesque of motifs
drawn from different projects – from the Devil's Glen wands,
the *Hamlet's Mill* turbine, from the letters of a 'Parrot Alphabet'
I devised in 2005 and from current thoughts about eddy forms
in Alice Springs. Notes adjacent to this figure discuss a book of
notes about the environment, conceived by analogy with Francis
Bacon's collection of experiments, his *Sylva sylvarum*. They ponder
the compositional logic of a miscellany –
a collection of observations that 'correspond to the state of
knowledge', leaving gaps where principles are unknown and in this
way causing the hidden and the incomplete also to appear and
take shape. Obviously, FIG 68 is not an illustration of this, but
the resemblance is clear:
a thought picture in this sense, it
serves to translate the topic of the
miscellaneous into a *topos*, or mental place
that can be visualised.

The connection between thinking, writing and drawing is also evident
in PLATE 30 where a taxonomy of involution accompanies a graphic
caprice composed of multiple volutes and turbines.

Drawings like this can be linked to more 'realistic' sketches –
the double spiral, for example, presented as another entrance marker
option in Alice Springs (FIGS 75, 76) – but their fascination with
pattern-making as such also links them to a number of 'arabesques'
or graphic mosaics that are explored purely for decorative effect
FIGS 74, 85, 86 fall into
this category.

Obviously akin to baroque
ornament generating an endless
effusion of organic shapes out
of the simplest, archetypal
prototypes, these scribbles
recognize no frame or organizing
principle beyond the impulse

75

74

76

to pattern.
They can achieve
formal identity and
closure (PLATE 28),

but except as a demonstration of the shape-forming potential of the
simplest motifs they mean nothing. In this context, I am reminded
of Edgar Allen Poe's observation in his introduction to
The Conchologist's First Book, that shells have a privileged
place in geognosy because
they bridge the organic
and inorganic worlds,
belonging equally
to biology and geology.

These scribbles are
similarly mineral and marine. The doodle, FIG 77 reminds me of Poe's
description of the structure of univalves: the 'Pillar, or columella,
is that *process* which runs through the centre of the shell in the inside
from the base to the apex of most univalve shells, and appears to be
the support of the spire.'[62]

Edgar Allan Poe, *The Conchologist's First Book*, Philadelphia: Haswell, Barrington & Haswell, 1839, 16. My italics.

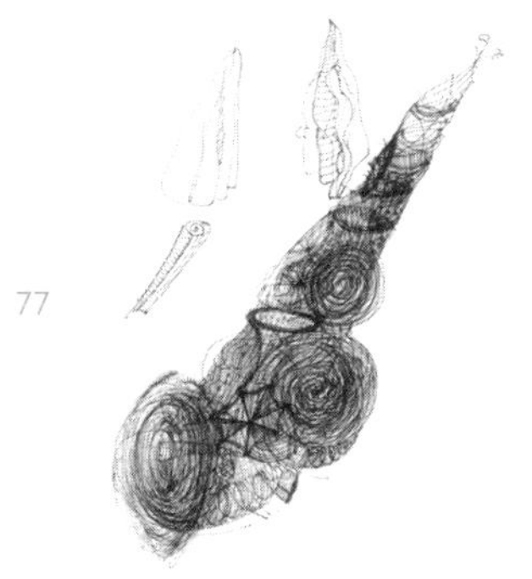

77

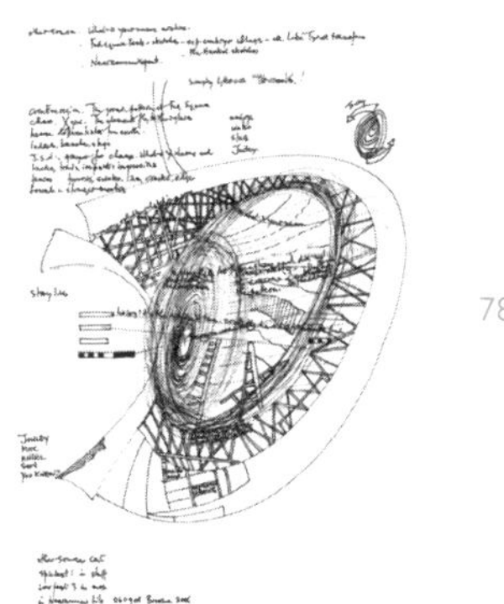

78

My sketch is a spire
in search of a pillar; and this may be a general criticism
of these notebook records, that they disguise a lack of formal clarity
or mastery with an enveloping cloud of graphic rotations,
cross-hatchings and other semblances of surface. The result is soft
forms,
involutes of movement,
instantly recognisable
but unstable and unlikely to be finished (See FIG 78, PLATE 29).

Like the scroll in FIG 79, they are palimpsestic structures born of
the erosion or correction of earlier passes; they grow like scar tissue
skin over the wound at the core; or insist that unaccomplished first
approximations can nevertheless be curated, amplified and
otherwise drawn out to provide a bridge or
scale to perfection.

79

7.

In a social context,

drawings like these can serve as talking points:
in the context of a place-making conversation,
they invite interpretation. They may not represent anything that can be
drawn up in CAD but they do suggest a process. They communicate
the formation of an idea, growing like the branches of the tree
through multiple overlays and revisions towards the outline of a
distinct region. As they are not linear drawings, so the interpretation
of them is not
linear: the story woven around them concerns
potential relationships and their materialisation
at that time and place.
Evoking a neighbourhood or archipelago
of energy forms, they also indicate
magnetic pathways between them.
As studies of interference patterns,
they hypothesise meeting places.

These meeting places are simultaneously conceptual – as when
a new metaphorical connection is grasped or a formal resemblance
recognised – and physical, suggesting the interest of the drawer in
certain spatial relationships, for none of these sketches is abstract
in the sense of

being

free of all dramaturgical desire. Physical meeting places are always driving the lines to interfold or turn away. The heuristic value, if you like, of these dawdling designs derives from the character of the patterns that emerge; that is, the organisational intelligence of the emerging drawing corresponding perhaps to the unknown algorithms governing the movement forms of sociability.

So, for example, when the global whorl pattern for *Nearamnew* was derived from the Lake Tyrrell bark etching, a form of sociability was attributed to it: the system of interlocking horseshoe forms suggested a crowd of curving paths or curvilinear trajectories mapping Levinas's possible

'paths of propinquity.'

On a couple of occasions, this generalised figure of encounter was, as it were, tested for its explanatory value. *Suspended Ground*, a work proposed for the fifth anniversary celebrations of the opening of Federation Square transformed the units of the global whorl pattern into components of a Calderesque mobile suspended from the ceiling of the Atrium (FIG 80). The image inevitably recalled Vico's theory of vortically-stacked historical *ricorsi*, as if the different curving inclines were fossilisations of earlier historical arrangements – whose collection here showed that they fitted into a larger involute of civilisational growth and change.

As a memory image of public space, *Suspended Ground* implied
an environmental unconscious, a palimpsest of earlier traces only
encountered through an act that replaces them; although successive
passages must wipe out the earlier tracks, they achieve this act
of historical amnesia by **walking faithfully in the tracks of
those who have gone before.** Here is the secret function
of design, to lay down those paths,

stairs,

terraces and doorways

that manage to express the choreographic intelligence of the region.

On another occasion,
I applied the global whorl pattern to the interpretation of neglected
story lines important in the history of the Mallee, the Victorian inland
where Lake Tyrrell is located. In the book *Ground Truthing* (2010), the
stories are told of two historical figures whose journeys through that
country must have criss-crossed. Unequivocal evidence of a meeting
between the Wotjobaluk man Jowley and the itinerant labourer
poet John Shaw Neilson is lacking; however, imagining their lives as
a palimpsest of all the journeys they ever made through that country,
a shared spatial history can be traced. **I imagined the journeys
as interlocking regions,
or as chiasmatically-related peripatetic circuits,
or even as slowly rotating regions nested inside**

regions.

The shaper of these different historical movement forms remained
the Lake Tyrrell bark etching, but the experiment of *Suspended
Ground* had let me see it extruded three dimensionally when its
separately moving but interlocked parts suggested the movement
of a cosmic clock – **a chronometer whose revolutions
express the differential rhythmic geography of the
region.**

Hence, in hybrid forms referencing both the *Pearl*
project and the *Nearamnew* derivatives represent the Tyrrell etching
as a three dimensional scroll, another palimpsestic device for rolling
the past into the convolutions of the present. In these drawings the
plot of a life is plotted; a direct connection is assumed
between telling a story and mapping a journey.
Further,
as the story lines of a life are not linear but zigzag,

                                   vortical,

                                   variably purposeful and

                                   durational,
the plot it creates is like a maze, more densely filled in here, less

                                   cross-hatched or detailed there.

In the case of *Suspended Ground* and *Ground Truthing*, I was
attributing a narrative significance to physical shapes: a jigsaw of
interlocking parts was read as if it were the trace
of many journeys
and
the places they made where they joined, passed
through one another or merged. But, obviously, you could
turn this process round: if stories can be made after their places, as
appears when the life lines of Jowley and Neilson are plotted using
the Lake Tyrrell template, so, in principle, a drawing of
a forming idea could foreshadow the emergence
of a place. There is, after all,
a natural
resemblance between
place-making stories
and places
made after their stories.

These drawings of movement forms could easily be interpreted as historical scores and, by extension,

as the kind of notation a storyteller might improvise in order to mark the successive twists and turns of the plot. Visualising the temporal structure of the story, they let you see all of the story at once, much in the way that the weaving of the carpet eventually produces a pattern to which all the threads contribute. In this way, the linear story, driving towards a definitive outcome, finds itself caught in a larger non-linear web where the meaning incorporates all the passages that have contributed to the pattern PLATES 37, 46.

As regards the life paths of historical characters like Jowley or John Shaw Neilson, when redrawn in this way their relationship with each other ceases to depend on a climactic meeting: it can be imagined instead as a site of convergence within the collective memory form – as if we were to derive individual experiences from the sum of all the eyes of the crowd, so that the map of their lives looked like a twinkling firmament through which

a shooting star fell.

As the habit of doodling grew, initially private sketches began to leak out into the meeting room. To explain ideas, I sometimes tabled a notebook sketch. Later, I began to doodle during the meetings, elaborating a patchwork maze that was perceived to be a diagram of our discourse: when a recognisable image floated to the surface of improvisations, it was received as the materialisation of a collective thought, a condensation of different mental ideations that proved the existence of common ground. So, again, plotting – making a plan – and plot as spatial enclosure were coterminous. But the important point was that these sketches did not drive towards linear

development or formal closure.

Our word *sketch* goes back to an older word, (Latin) *schedium*, meaning an extemporised poem, in turn related to Greek *skhedios* with the sense of 'temporary' or 'made off-hand'; drawing of this kind is simultaneously verbal and gestural. In *Neglected Dimensions*, the connection is even closer as the purpose of extemporisation is place-making. But the difference, again, is plain: instead of enclosing space and fixing concepts, the doodle that draws together the threads of conversation attributes significance to the to and fro of discourse. The spatio-temporal discontinuity of this design can be compared to the 'nondirected linearity' of certain recent music which 'moves by a variety of means

and with varying degrees of localised stability

at cadences, yet it avoids the implication that certain pitches can

become totally stable.'[63]

Jonathan D. Kramer, 'New Temporalities in Music,' *Critical Enquiry*, 7 (3), Spring 1981, 539-556, 542.

Closer still in spirit are musical works that operate with

'moment time':

'Whereas a composition in multiple time has a clear beginning (or several unmistakable beginnings), which may

or may not occur at the start of the piece, a work in moment time does not really begin; rather, it simply starts, as if it had been going on all along and we happened to tune in on it.'[64]

Kramer, 'New Temporalities in Music,' 547.

In terms of drawing, any departure from the pure outline imitative of a fixed object introduces temporality into the design. As soon as the line ceases to be an exact copy of a pre-existing form, it introduces the quality of emergence. Discontinuous with the ideal form or presence, it proposes an alternative reality or organisation of space; it introduces volume, a sense of composition in the round;

and it incorporates
the coexistence of multiple temporalities
(or movement forms)
into the accumulating complexity of the pattern
(itself a function of the duration of the drawing process).

It would be surprising if this improvisatory mode did not produce distinctive outcomes or disclose personal interests. For instance, the hinge and pivot forms of *Hamlet's Mill* integrate multiple temporalities – to which they give different shapes. **The endless opening of Parmenides's Gates of Dawn suggests time passing on the spot,** a historical plot that grows deeper simply by attending to the dynamics of passage. The best drawing of the knowledge this situation produces remains Leonardo's 'Studies of an Old Man Seated and of Swirling Water,' whose 'eddying whirlpools' illustrate movement as feedback.[65]

In a related context, Paul Virilio writes, 'If the rapid shuttle is the perfect illustration of the constant feedback of our now globalized Time, the pivot of the pulley would then represent the axis of a Time belonging to a reason that tries to disclose the hidden meaning of the Event.'[66]

'... [T]hus the water forms eddying whirlpools, one part of which is due to the impetus of the principal current and the other to the incidental motion and return flow.' (A.E. Popham, *The Drawings of Leonardo di Vinci*, London: Jonathan Cape, 1971, 155.)

Paul Virilio, 'Foreword,' John Rajchman, *Constructions*, Cambridge, Mass. : The MIT Press, 1999, vi-viii, vii.

That is, in simple terms, the plot thickens when place is replaced with an act of **hollowing out**. The eddies, always on the point of disappearing, materialize the lost threads of a volume that envelops us.

8.

A paradox
lies at
the heart
of urban
design.

So far as public space design is concerned, designers rely on the validity of scaling up models. Whether studying the physical models of a place or interpreting CAD-generated imagery, they back their capacity to project the spatial logic inscribed into these figures accurately into the shaping of social life. Different tools of representation assume different capacities: a model is a working device for the identification of mechanical difficulties and the appreciation of aesthetic form; CAD drawings have the same relation to experience as films, and assume we can translate visual effects into imagined bodies and masses encountered in everyday experience.

If,
however,
Giacometti's insight is correct – that the situation of human encounter is scaleless – urban designers are profoundly misled when they imagine their drawing and modelling can accurately evoke those places that these days planners cheerfully characterise as fostering sociability. It is likely that what can be scaled up or miniaturised are precisely those dimensions of shared space and time that are immune to the solicitations of Eros, the Public Worker. At any rate, the neglected dimensions of political co-existence, which include all aspects of the movement form, as well as the stickiness of living compositions, ceaselessly forming and unforming, remain undescribed. An empty stage for action is prepared but the social script, the plot, remains unwritten.

The enigma of scale is also apparent in all manifestations of talk about place. One response to the problem of representation is the public consultation; usually conducted by telephone or on-line, a survey of community expectations is conducted.

Often, an impressive number of responses are collected, and from these data a list of desirable attributes can be derived. But the bias of these surveys is well-known: participants tend to be outspoken advocates of partial interests and, in any case, the measures of sociability integral to its achievement (everything associated with atmosphere and its constituents) are neither mentioned nor calculated.

At a more intimate scale, discussions between the political representatives of the public interest, Indigenous custodians and other place experts, and the design team are entirely about imagined communities and their imagined behaviours in public space; apart from well-known practitioners of socially-inclusive landscape design such as Jan Gehl, statistically-valid observations of public behaviour play a limited role in these discussions. With a surprising lack of self-consciousness, participants extrapolate from personal history to general principle. Like communities who for lack of the right lexicon are said to be unable to describe certain aspects of their world, speakers in this situation often seem surprisingly unable to articulate a sense of place.

I find the discourse of planned place-making alters when stories are told: when figurative language is used, poetic connections in language are made. Associations open up that are felt intuitively but which elude the language of administration; at least in the design concept and development phase, the capacity to make persuasive comparisons, discover hidden analogies and symbolic resonances exercises a strange fascination, as if the poetic overlay compensates for the anomie or human meaninglessness of the plan or design as such.

But I have also noticed that much opens up for discussion when *the tenor of the conversation itself* is annotated, as the interplay of different opinions or subject-positions may yield more knowledge of the kind of communication characteristic of public life than the opinions expressed. Further, the game of the dialogue, erotic in its release of creativity, may be an accurate rehearsal of the kind of situation that the designers imagine themselves designing. If, instead of supposing a singular place or meeting place is under discussion, a multitude of meeting places is imagined, as many *tourbillons* or tiny vortices in the public movement form as there exist groups ceaselessly forming and unforming, then no scaling up is required to establish the validity of the process.

If places are made after their stories, it is discourse that needs to be reformed; when poetry's power to draw together distant ideas is entertained, the linear perspective of visualism and the authority of quantitative data collection tend to evaporate.

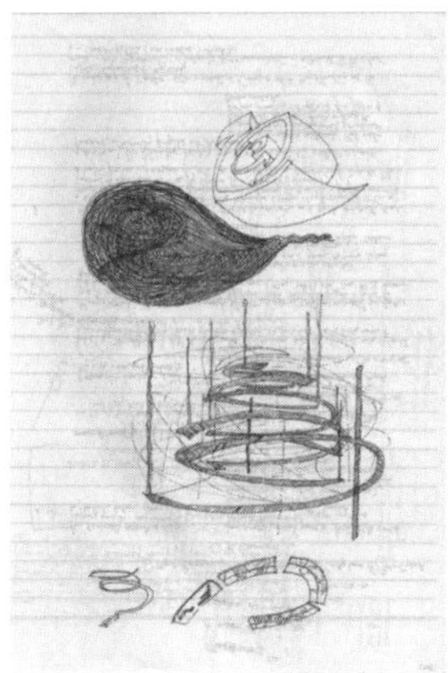

As I say, more recently, I have tried to map the to and fro of these kinds of professional and public consultation by drawing doodles during the meeting. Sometimes the results are tabled; sometimes they are retained and added to over the coming days, eventually finding their way into a proposal or report. Sketches like FIG 86, also PLATES 31-34, have been generated in this way.

Such *sketches* are not impartial records of meetings, graphic diagrams representing, say, the warp and weft of ideas exchange and an emergent fabric. They are extemporised expressions of what I was trying to describe, of what I was hearing others say in response and,

sometimes, of what I wished would appear (either as a topic or
as a place). Rather than refer to ideal objects or landscapes that can
be documented and built, they refer to passages, again understood
in their double sense, rhetorical and physical,

in-between.   as spaces

Just as the meaning of a conversation
may emerge through the gymnastic itself, the choreography of the
speaking positions mattering more than the views expressed,
so with a place: it may consist entirely of openings to the other and
the passages in-between that join these up. In this case, they evoke
chiasmatic movement forms, histories of passage and their vortical
accumulation around predetermined centres. They present places
as compositions, successfully reconciling or placing together,
heterogeneous elements; the compositional principle informing
this is not jigsaw-like but energetic,

> a sense of flow inducing whatever
> lies in its path to align until,
> through a growing feedback effect,
> a field or quilt
> of interrelated events is produced.

PLATE 32 is a sketch produced in this way.
The word *kelp* embedded in the landscape of the drawing identifies
this as belonging to a cultural heritage-into-urban design project
undertaken in Warrnambool (Victoria, Australia) between 2012-2014.
Given that this project generated such matter-of-fact documents
as 'Hidden Histories: laneway options' (a comprehensive assessment
of the informal network of 'capillary' passages woven into the
Warrnambool city grid) and 'Hidden Histories: a public art and
spaces strategy,' recommending that 'public art commissions should
be integrated functionally, culturally and aesthetically into

Warrnambool's public space design principles and practices,' one
could be forgiven for thinking that this sketch betrays the same crisis
Paul Klee experienced when he could not make his lines 'come out':
'I could not see them around me, the accord between
inside and outside was so hard to achieve.'[67]

Quoted in Carter, *Dark Writing*, 79.

Any connection with a planning scheme or a public art strategy is not
obvious. On the other hand, even if this volute composition

described
neglected dimensions of place experience, it did manage
an accord between inside and outside – as the names of the
exhibition,

Kelp

(Warrnambool Art Gallery, 8 May-8 June, 2014)

and the laneway public art proposal,

Kelp Lip

(July 2014) might indicate.

Or, perhaps more accurately, rather than find an accord, all of
these schemes (the 'inner' sketch and the 'outer' exhibit and
proposal) sought to give value to the divide itself, the chiasmatic
littoral zone where inside and outside were ceaselessly flowing in
out of each other. In the exhibition proposal the point was made that
'Warrnambool's coast is not a narrow line but a gathering and
interweaving of many interrelated habitats that lies on a spectrum
between wet and dry: deep sea,

> coastal shelf,
> offshore reefs,
> sandbanks,
> islands,
> isthmuses,
> intertidal expansions and contractions of shore

and associated appearance and disappearance of

        navigable channels,

        estuarine sandbars,

        mudflats,

        shifting river and creek mouths,

            beaches,

            rocky outcrops,

            extracts of cliffs with fallen

boulders,

            hummocks of sand,

            pools,

            fresh water,

            more or less defined creeks

leading into and out of swamps,

            wetlands,

            morasses,

            sandy soil,

            firmer ground,

            conglomerate,

            ground cover,

            ti-tree,

            low bush,

            stands of mallee-like gum,

            sandy valleys and hills

(ancient coastlines) with stringybark,

            richer soils in places,

            limestone ridges,

            fallen timber and stands of

native cypress …

            and eventually lava.'

The complexity of this transition was mirrored in the history of human discourse - the hidden history of this unique coastal environment was 'contained in the translations between English, Irish and other European languages and the 'kelp lip' language of

the local Gundidjmara people that brought it into being: between sea and land, between languages and cultures. Warrnambool is a speaking place, where sounds spilled out of human lips to become the names of things, relationships, hopes and fears ...' In some sense, PLATE 34 could be said to express the *feel* of this expanded edge, littoral (belonging to the environment)
and

                               literal (belonging to the inscription of voices) .

The concept of an expanded edge emerged again through engagements in Western Australia. Nyungar understandings of the spiritual and social protocols governing admission to their country played an important role in the public art and interpretation strategies for Yagan Square (Perth) and for Scarborough Beach (north-west of Perth). In the course of developing a 'creative template' to guide art and design decisions in the Scarborough Beach Redevelopment, I emphasized the value of regarding the iconic surf beach as an 'expanded edge,' where the line was reinterpreted as the traveling front of the wave and the parallel crestings of the sand dunes; there were also north-south movement ways that could be compared to the transverse *dérive* of the surfer or the footsteps of Aboriginal people seasonally travelling the country. Whatever new infrastructure was proposed should be conceived like wave-sculpted water, as standing amid ceaseless motion. Addressed here was the same stillness/motion paradox characteristic of the Parmenidean gate, or of any stable movement form.

To express the feel of the expanded edge, I drew PLATE 33. When its vision was explained to government planners, it became surprisingly legible.

It could never furnish a landscape design
or an interpretation strategy but its warp and weft, its duplication
of waterspouts,

twisting ramparts,

hollowed ranks and

zoomorphic water spirits,

suggested a place of chameleon-like formal transformation. While
nothing was represented, the energetic patterning of the beach was
conveyed, a certain metabolic intensity or dynamic atmosphere that
should be secured. That this should resemble a dream was not
accidental: it recalls us to the night time of the
imagination,

the land of those who have gone before and of those who are to come.

Prior to working at Scarborough,

I had explored the creative
possibilities of movement forms in the development of Yagan Square,
Perth. It is customary to begin with the consultation of Aboriginal
interests, accessed directly through discussion and indirectly
through ethnographic sources and cultural writings of all kinds.
In the central Perth Yagan Square design and the Scarborough Beach
Redevelopment project, formal consultative arrangements between
the government planning agency and the Nyungar community meant
that the usual gap between cultural heritage and urban design could
be greatly narrowed.

An illustration of this has been the interpretation through the
public art program of the Nyungar term *waullu*, recorded in George
Fletcher Moore's early account of the Noongar Language, where it
is defined as 'Light;

> dawn;
>
> daylight;
>
> the morning twilight;
>
> the interval between light and darkness;
>
> a clear open space without trees;
>
> an interval or open space between two objects;
>
> the division of the hair, when parted on the top

of the head; partial baldness.' [68]
The association with
'the division of the
hair' suggested that the term *waullu* could be imagined spatially:
a temporal hinge moment ('the interval between light and darkness')
could be imagined as a passage opening up in the act of passing.
Such a passage was not a permanent place or structure –
not another kind of *bidi*, the Nyungar term for *path*, to be conceived
as the theatre or container that passage left behind. It was
passing as gerund, a state of becoming, if you like,
imagined
as a line being drawn,

drawn out.

In the public artwork *Passenger* at Yagan Square, the spatio-temporal
concept of *waullu* was connected to the story of a Nyungar woman,
Fanny Balbuk, who resisted the growth of the colonial city by
insisting on taking the old paths to her gathering grounds even when
these passed straight through fences and walls. [69]
The figure of Balbuk was imagined as a silhouette or outline,
a palpable absence driving through the walls and steps of the new city
square (FIG 87). The idea of presenting an absence positively went back
to the operation of Bunjil's *Ber-rang*, as well as recalling the 'asterisk
principle' developed at Victoria Harbour. Here it also revisited
the paradox of the Parmenidean gate, still but moving.

[68] G.F. Moore, *A Descriptive Vocabulary of the Language in Common Use amongst the Aborigines of Western Australia.* London: Wm. S. Orr & Co., 1842, 103.

[69] Carter, *Places Made After Their Stories,* 351-353.

PLATES 34 and 41 are, in this context, classic involutes, palimpsests of
earlier movement forms (asterisks, lattices, silhouettes). Such designs
assert the existence of movement forms, hollows or partings that
open up in the midst; although almost impossible to fix and
represent, they may be the neglected dimension of place-making
that creates a sense of atmosphere or *milieu*. Amplifying the seeming
paradox of a place that simultaneously contracts to a vanishing point
and expands to envelop us entirely, Serres compares the 'mid-place
[*mi-lieu*] of a square to a diagonal dividing a square in two.
Unlike the sides of the square, 'which it separates in two without
a middle [*milieu*] imposing itself on intuition. It exists then, but it
is ineffable.' [70]
The diagonal is a line that connects the inner and the outer, the
infinitely small and the inexpressibly large.

Michel Serres, *The Troubadour of Knowledge*, trans S.F. Glaser & W. Paulson, Ann Arbor: University of Michigan Press, 1997, 43.

*W*aullu is like this. It is another device for overcoming the
problem of scale: like the horizon, an action adjusted to its environment, it is right wherever it is. Running parallel to the coastline, it
reconfigures the coastline as a 'diagonal' in Michael Serres's sense:
absurd, impossible to name, from this fissure in reality the
pronouncement of the ineffable becomes possible. As an item
transferred from the realm of cultural heritage to kinesthetic
experience,

it exemplifies poetic place-making.

Mystic Edge, the artwork that emerged from this insight
was envisaged as a choreotopographical device,
articulating the feedback between human movement
and the character of the redeveloped landscape,
acting, in this context, as a kind of amplifier
or repeater of rhythms set up between
the passage of people and
the arabesque of the ground plane.

Nyungar elder, Richard Walley, told me that *waullu* meant both parting *and meeting*. An opening, interval or open space between two points, it can also be understood as the action of people walking in two directions, continuously meeting,

passing and parting. It is a figure of linear sociability, somewhat like

the breaking edge of the wave that endlessly renews itself (FIG 81) .

81

Where two people walking in opposite directions pass one another, V-shaped wakes spread through each other, creating diamond-shaped interference patterns (PLATE 35). Out of contrary impulses self-distorting and transforming complexities multiply (FIGS 81-82). The multiplication of paths, the distraction of intentions from the straight and narrow path dear to planners, expresses the paradox at the heart of meeting - the experience of non-meeting. (PLATE 33). Surfers explain that the 'mysto edge' alluded to in the name *Mystic Edge*, is 'a surf spot that breaks on a far away reef,' a line of foam unzipping out to sea that the surfer cannot reach,

82

83

a wave
that can
never be
ridden.

9.

Can such doodles contribute anything of practical value to the interrelated activities of urban planning and redevelopment, the cultural repatriation of environments and the socio-political goals of democratic mobility, inclusion and value exchange? Specialisations exist to define, map and monitor these domains; entire schools and departments support the development and refinements of techniques and protocols aimed at managing local, regional and national infrastructure. The same political mechanisms that facilitate social change and support technological innovation inhibit the application of rough, messy practices of place-making as too risky, controversial or insufficiently predictable to warrant investment.

We say these are sketches of 'movement forms' but, unlike Leibniz's vision of a calculus able to find the line that runs through all possible points, these 'points' are fat, revolutionary and dendritic; constitutionally distributed, they gain nothing by being reduced to an algorithmic function governing change. Nor can we ride on the coattails of fractal physics: recursive in the simplest sense that lines go over themselves at different scales, these caprices lack both the skill and the appetite to study enigmas of scaling (PLATE 36).

A scan of PLATE 38 was included in the exhibition *Descriptions* in Adelaide in 2003. To contextualize it, I wrote at the time, 'A notebook entry adjacent to this drawing reads in part: 'The track is the mobile aspect of the blot. It is the *drag* between *macchie* … Just as the agora is a widening of the track, so the track is a concentration of the gathering place. The track is like the tilted jug from which liquid pours. The *macchia* is the deepening, spreading stain of that inclination. In describing ground writing this dialogue between track and spot is essential: the writing line is not a smooth arabesque, nor does it approach a regular network. It is a broken pattern lent accent by the location, the pull and lean of the knots.' And I called the sketch 'Meeting Places.' As an incubator of sociability, public space is imagined here as a quilt composed of multiple centres of attraction, the whole held together like a string figure by the forces also pulling it apart.

Applications of this idea occur in *Tracks* (FIG 41), in *Solution* (PLATE 1) and *Golden Grove* (PLATE 15). Writing about the layout of the nodal points in *Golden Grove*, for example, I noted, 'The arrangement of the stars in the Pleiades cluster furnished us with the nodal points of a spreading ground pattern. The important thing about the Pleiades as a constellation is not that they form nine isolated points but that they are a field of lights subtly joined by "filaments". Perhaps for this reason Indigenous paintings show them as a solid field of twinkling spheres. Further, from Galileo forward, the Pleiades have been drawn as if they were composed of two elements – a long curving path or tail and an uncoiling spiral.'[71]

Carter, *Places Made After Their Stories*, 169.

The units or crossing places of PLATE 38 could equally well be
compared to the compartments of an Aboriginal possum cloak,
each of which bears a different pattern. Those different patterns are
said to symbolise different patches of country: my sketch suggests
a loosely gridded system of flows and catchments. Common to both
is a federal organization where the patching embodies a principle
of outpouring not containment.[72]

Carter, *Places Made After Their Stories*, 398-408.

In a characteristically Australian lacework or anastomosing
waterflow system the distinction between channels and pools is
lost: in the distributed meeting place, composed with the threads
of *waullu*, as it were, its continual weaving together depends on a
back-and-forth rhythm of openings and partings. Benoit Mandelbrot
who coined the term fractal is said to have first become interested
in the mathematics of dynamic systems through his fascination with
maps and his parents' oriental rugs.

Perhaps the key point here is that rugs exhibit both symmetry
and symmetry-breaking: when a different colour than expected is
used or the same colour is used in a different location, the symmetry
is broken and, in the hands of the master weaver, repetitive
patterns may be transformed into great works of art.[73]

See for example Carol Bier, 'Weaving Infinity: Symmetry in Islamic Carpets', *Symmetry*, vol. 19, nos. 2 & 3, 2008, 199-219.

But this can work the other way round, and non-symmetrical
patterns in nature can be woven into designs whose symmetry
signifies the symbolic palimpsest that intertwines different scales of
creation. For example, Ngarrindjeri weaver Ellen Trevorrow, and her
daughter, have used the same constellation invoked in *Golden Grove*,
in 2002 exhibiting a work called 'Mat and Seven Sister Baskets',
'This particular work refers to a traditional Ngarrindjeri story about
the Seven Sisters constellation. The story encodes Ngarrindjeri beliefs
about the formation of the world which is here expressed in woven
form. It also symbolised family relationships. The sister baskets were

made

by Ellen and the mat was made by her daughter, Tanya, reconnecting
the passing on of inter-generational knowledge.' Ellen Trevorrow
refers to herself as a 'cultural weaver.'[74]

Kay Lawrence, 'Weaving an encounter between the Njarrinderjeri, the British and the French,' at http://w3.unisa.edu.au/hawkecentre/events/2002events/encounter_weaving.asp

Weaving a rug or basket is different from sewing together
a patchwork quilt. In weaving, the frame or loom establishes an
artificial plan, somewhat like a map projection, and the
pattern is progressively discovered through repeated traverses.
In *Alterations*, a ground pattern and associated program for what
became known as Harmony Square, Dandenong (south-east of
Melbourne), a hybrid technique was used: patterns derived from
fabrics sold locally were collaged together (sewn) into a patchwork;
then the pattern was subjected to iterative redrawing until (like the
completed pattern of a woven cloth) the motif was found.[75] (FIG 84)

Carter, *Places Made After Their Stories*, 244-254.

84

In the context of place-making, though, the difference between
weaving and sewing need not be overdrawn. What may count more is
the animation of the surface, the recognition of the material, whether
animal skin or cotton, as the garment of the earth, folding and
unfolding in the walk of the seasons and of geological eons. Laid
over the body of the earth, patterns bunch or stretch
out and fold together in unexpected ways; strange
Rorschach-like symmetries occur, then fade away.
In this recombination the mobile body writes back, weaving new
patterns into the collage and dissolving the fixed symmetries
of the textile.

Contemporary discourse about urban renewal,
invigorated landscape design, the form and function of public art

invariably invokes weaving as its primary criterion of sociability.
In its simplest form, the notion of walkers weaving in and out of each
other's paths – that vernacular choreography we practice
everyday – is perceived as a therapeutic alternative to the linear
progress which linear design encourages.

An economy is tied to this: for the business-like walker with
deadlines to meet,

> the knots,
>
> loops,
>
> errancies and
>
> deviations of weaving a path through others represent

a waste of time. For the figure who has no other business, however,
errancy is not a form of loitering, but the means of making room.
Errancy is not directionless but is to be compared
with the method of weaving. Both are inconceivable without
the other, whether the other is a stranger or the second
yarn. Even when the fabric is woven from a single thread, its extent
is a function of the knots that hold it open. In the same way, the sum
of all the paths we have taken form a pattern that has a structure of its
own, a regularity and a history.

This much is theoretically clear – but how little of it
comes out in drawing practice: the landscapes of the designers are
silent,
unpeopled,
linear;
even their animations propel ghosts down straight lines. In this
context, pattern making, whatever its technique, is less a method for
scoring public space and more an accompaniment of storytelling (or
yarning). 'It is beautiful to sit and weave while you yarn together,'
says Ellen Trevorrow; and I have found something similar as
I have learned to doodle while we talk. Drawings produced while
a conversation is proceeding back and forth across a room of different
but related

positions are, as I say, not representations of that warp and weft, but
they could be said to discover a pattern
or emergent form (FIG 85).

Translating lines of thought
into stripes,

           patches
or

                  fields,
they can discover hidden geometries
in the conversation,

unnamed,
overlooked
or
negative spaces

at the heart of the spoken, that haunt the facts like
hearsay (FIG 86)

In the case of *Rival Channels*, a sculptural mural inspired by the flow
and counterflow of the Brisbane River (PLATE 39), the analogy is
reversed: an attempt to evoke the movement form of the river as
a bi-directional turbulence pattern created a figure that conjured
up the Brownian motion of urban life,

a history of
unfinished
encounter
or even a
graphic
palimpsest
of dialogues
repeatedly left
off and started
again
.

10.

Another way

in which these sketches come out is in the CAD drawings that my son produces.

I have always appreciated this father-son communion through drawing as professionally remarkable and precious. In Edmund's interpretation rough sketches become polished models, two dimensional (or obscurely dimensioned entanglements of lines) are resolved into sculptural objects that are topologically possible even when their physical construction might defy logic. Drawing together signifies in this instance a dialogue occasioned by an idea of mine – a sketch – whose translation into a digital object clarifies the (usually) invisible impulse or the movement form inspiring the lines. Able to manipulate and transform a sculptural object, we can quickly populate a field with poses, combined and recombined figures that visualise a formal meeting place.

This might suggest that the drawings in this book fall into two groups: those that can yield figures that can be built and those that remain resolutely conceptual or musical (they can be copied but not three dimensionalised). But, in reality, the distinction is often blurred: the act of redrawing a hand sketch in CAD may extract a previously unimagined

object

from the graphic flux, while, in the other direction, watching the most speculative of gestures generate a new system of pattern-making fosters a new awareness of what meaningless doodles may mean. Some of the most inscrutable patchworks of lines may, after all, be further variations on parametrically-generated patterns, inspired by the seemingly limitless power to metabolise formerly fixed and stilted forms.

Here, though, the personal relationship is more important. Ellen Trevorrow reflects, 'I like weaving with the old people because they yarn about things, the past, which is the future for their children. Sometimes they tell secrets it's good to share and exchange.' [76]

Lawrence, 'Weaving an encounter between the Njarrinderjeri, the British and the French.'

Something similar happens in the weaving of threads between father and son; a yarning occurs that may be largely composed of gestures and almost wordless, a communication centred on pointing out an emerging pattern. The pattern is the secret handed over; discovered together, it establishes a bond between us. The techniques employed in achieving this shared sense of discovery are less important than the exploratory drawing itself.

The graphic projection
of eidetic interests
creates a shared memory place,
one that lends biography or life
writing new *graphic* meaning.

Perhaps this is especially important in a migrant family, where father and son have grown up in different places – where the past is not the future of their children, but another country. Outside of the family home, their senses of place are likely to be profoundly different. The Pegasus-leap of the imagination that propelled the father here is a stride that may leave no trace in the consciousness of the child. The son's eidetic reservoir comes from another generation of imagery, another training and other associations. The fit that is felt when the elements of a pattern or a figure come together is **like**

a meeting place where strangers approaching from a great distance find how much they have in common.

In a series called *Hinges*, I returned with my son to Uffington White Horse in Berkshire, England, close to where I grew up. We did this remotely, using photographs I had recently taken there. We created stencils from the different parts of the late Bronze Age hill figure and laid these over movement forms, ground patterns developed for different public art and design projects. The idea was to see whether any discernible eido-kinetic *Gestalt* linked the playground of my childhood to the choreographies I characteristically sketched here: 'Paintings, drawings and even sculptures are not transparent representations: their images emerge from a labyrinth of tracks produced by the brush, the fingers and indeed the whole choreography of the artist's interaction with his materials. The sign of this labyrinthine, pre-imaginal history is the face or look of the work. And this appeals to us because we possess an eido-kinetic intuition, and therefore recognize that the "gulf" in the look, the instant between two strides, and indeed the entire "interruption" of the artwork, models the kingdom of gaps in which we live.'[77]

Certainly, this pre-imaginal interaction with the world offers a genuine biographical insight. 'It is this primary passage between one state and the other that foreshadows the vicissitudes of the Ego's later dealings with the world, and whose fusion characterizes the satisfying artwork whatever its explicit subject-matter: "Formal relationships themselves entail a representation of imagery of their own though these likenesses are not as explicit as the image we obtain from what we call the subject-matter"[78],' I wrote quoting Adrian Stokes, but also noting that 'The Ego-figure' in Stokes's thesis is 'an epitome of balance or stable corporeality,'[79] whereas the figure I am invoking is always caught mid-stride, shuttling between different positions.'

[77] This experiment is described in Paul Carter, 'Masters of the gap: art, migration and eido-kinesis,' in *After the Event: New perspectives on art history*, eds. C. Merewether & J. Potts, Manchester: Manchester University Press, 2010, 43-56, 48.

[78] Adrian Stokes, *Greek Culture and the Ego*. London: Tavistock Press, 1958, 52.

[79] Stokes, *Greek Culture and the Ego*, 9.

Looking back at this experiment, though, the focus shifts:
originally framed as a chapter in a biography conceived spatially,
I recognize it now as mapping common ground between father and
son. The blending of images achieved in Photoshop was a power to
eliminate incommensurable origins. Able to adjust,

orientate,

scale up and scale down

the stencils, it was inevitable that correspondences would be found
with the selected art imagery. An extract of a drawing for *Nearamnew*
fitted into the neck of the Horse; one of the *Golden Grove* nodes or
star points easily peeped out through the eye of the Horse; an arch
of dancing figures developed for an unrealized project called *Pivotal*
paraded round the boomerang of the Horse's back leg.

Having found – or manipulated the materials to produce –
correspondences, the principle or hypothesis that certain corporeal
measures of social space were remembered and carried over could be
applied analytically. Through the stencil of the White Horse other
visual documentation for projects could be examined for their
movement forms. Pathways,

distributions,

arrangements,

interference patterns suggestive of shared rhythmic
geographies could be isolated.

But the value of fusing these pre- and post-migration
choreographies was, I see now, largely transactional, an eidetic game
of hide-and-seek played out in the present. It opened up a space
between father and son, a discursive domain that used spatial figures
metaphorically to give to patterns a new sense of historical place and
personal meaning.

87

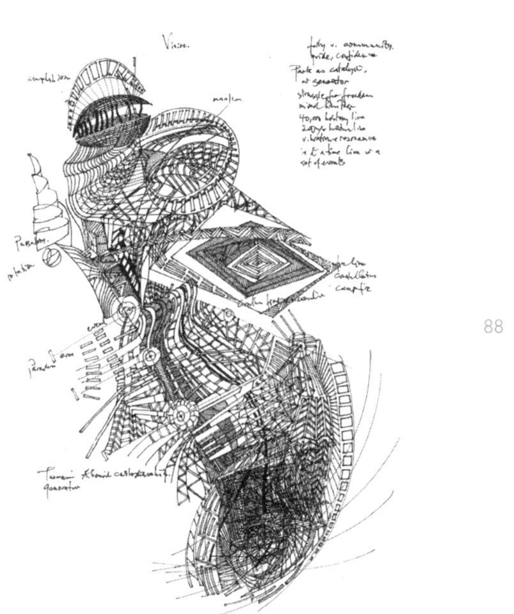

88

II.

An interesting

dilemma arose recently in relation to an Indigenous heritage interpretation trail proposed for the ocean-edge suburb of Scarborough in Western Australia.

It concerned the absence of a strong Nyungar graphic tradition. The proposal was to create five ground figures representing five episodes in a foundational mythological narrative that had strong associations with the area. The question immediately arose of intelligibility: even the classic Western Desert art 'dot-and-circle' compositions associated with Geoffrey Bardon's residency at Papunya in 1970-71 depend on the artist's verbal explanation for their deeper understanding. The artist team involved did not want to fall back on Central Australian stereotypes but faced the delicate challenge of inventing their own Nyungar symbols.

At first this presented itself as a problem of recognition: how could the new 'language' of symbols be read by the community when no one was familiar with it? But gradually it became clear that any system of visual symbols, even one widely disseminated, must fall short of diegetic expectation. It emerged that the root of the problem lay in the artificial distinction that the permanent installation implied between storyteller and drawing, between telling the story and marking its characters and actions in the sand. The standard division in western art between image and text places an unusual pressure on the artist to compose scenes naturalistically; on the *ut pictura poesis* principle, the storyteller qua graphic performer finds the presentation of psychological states or causal connections almost impossible.

Involvement in the subsequent design process led me to reflect on the similar problem presented by the sketches or doodles collected here. Any verbal exegesis of their meaning is bound to be an act of translation, the figuring forth in another medium (language) of a figure whose internal logic and immediate historical context are either obscure or forgotten. Unsupported by any conventional symbolic language, they borrow eclectically from topographical drawing, informal mimetic sketching practices, 'action' drawing where the gesture directly describes the movement form and various kinds of cartoon or study that possess a dream clarity but no obvious application FIG 86.

From time to time in this narrative I have sought to contextualize sketches by referring to adjacent hand writing: the Australian notebooks consist largely of ideas and observations made in the course of collecting materials for books or creative projects, they are, as Francis Bacon might say, a *sylva sylvarum*, or miscellany of experimental materials laid together against the future construction of an ordered edifice. In visualizing different kinds of construction, the drawings are in this sense illustrative.

But what is equally plain is that the adjacent writings yield poorly: exterior data about place and project may be conveyed and, very often, a scattering of concepts; in general, though, the match is poor. Some of the drawings must have taken days or weeks of casual revisiting to achieve their present form. In that period, the moving finger, having writ, moved on; but even when the information catchment is widened to include dates significantly preceding or postdating the drawing, the informational yield remains meagre.

In understanding the relationship between drawing and writing, diagrams and diegetics, a different approach may be more useful. Many of the doodles are drawn over writing; others incorporate letters and words; and yet others are composed of letters (PLATE 40). In many cases writing bleeding through from the other side of the page provides a ghost template, whose formality is reinforced where the pages of the notebook are lined. In short, the *design* relationship between drawing and writing is stronger than the discursive one.

A focus of the majority of public artworks alluded to in *Neglected Dimensions – Nearamnew, Golden Grove* - has been writing in public space: the development of customized fonts, adaptation of concrete poetry techniques, and borrowing from Lettriste hypergraphics characterize these typographical landscapes. But their prototype, the experimental template where many of these arrangements have first been imagined may be the white rectangle of the notebook page, where it often looks as if the casual jottings scattered over the page provide the essential catalyst, the vestigial archipelago or incipient arrangement that gets the re- luctant doodler 'over the line,' persuaded to start joining up the little arabesques into something larger.

Certainly, it appears rare for my cursive scrawls to postdate the sketches; they belong to the archaeology of the project, strange scriptural attractors licensing a region of graphic invention.

Some of the earlier sketches were compared to topographical *esquisses,* perspectival caprices suggestive of erosive landscapes defined by networks of flowpaths, but they could equally be read as imaginary topics rather than topoi. FIGS 4, 43, 44, 86, 87, for example, arrange patterns on the page in the same way that, elsewhere, I have arranged paragraphs. In PLATES 31 and 32 the translation between theme (topic) and mental place (topos) are easily observed. The raked perspectives of these and other drawings refers to the temporal ordering of space in writing as much as any convention of topographical representation: western script is read from left to right and from top to bottom. The composition of a page of writing takes its cues from the opening gestures: the scale of the script, the selection of left and right margins, the decision (in my case) to write on or in-between the lines, not to mention the colour of the texta ink used: these visual signatures inaugurate a page composed to fulfil an aesthetic as well as a writerly function (see lines and bleed-through FIG 80).

Nor is the ornamentation of the page exterior to its meaning. When the aphorisms or passages assembling on the page can be lent a formal spatial patterning I am more persuaded of their ultimate creative significance. In achieving clarity something depends on the quality of the thought but much on the crispness and flow of the pen tip.

These preoccupations have ancient origins. Greek letters were known as *stoicheia, stoichein* being used alike for the letter and the sound it represented. As *stoichos* means a row or rank of units, *stoicheion* means a single unit in the row. Aristophanes called the shadow of the sundial gnomon *stoicheion.* In relation to the *stoichedon* style in Greek inscriptions, Carson discusses the chequerboard incised into the stone's surface, providing the matrix for fixing the position of the letters, and cites the inscription on the so-called stele of Moschion (2-3rd C AD; Egypt), commenting,

'The simile in these lines refers to the irrigation of a field laid out in small squares.' These letters 'aligned vertically as well as horizontally and placed at equal intervals along their respective alignments like ranks of men in military formation,' were, she suggests, read (and presumably composed) like a crossword puzzle.[80]

Anne Carson, *Economy of the Unlost: Reading Simonides of Keos with Paul Celan*, Princeton: Princeton University Press, 2002, 49.

These precedents resonated when I began to think typo-graphically, transposing the informal compositional principles of the notebook page to the larger page of public space, where ranks of letter had to be organized vertically and horizontally and, ideally, a correspondence was sensed between the arrangement and the meaning.

In fact, it may be that these fused pages where telling the story and printing it in stone have equal value reintegrate practices that have drifted apart but which were anciently interchangeable. In this case, the comparison with Aboriginal calligraphic practices not only has cross-cultural historical value but implications for contemporary practice. The idea that speaking and drawing can go together was commonplace in Etruscan times – where 'the palette and the alphabet were often the complementary tools of the art of signifying and symbolizing.'[81]

Francesco Roncalli, 'Painting,' in *The Etruscans*, ed. M. Torelli, Milan: Bompiani, 2000, 345-364, 345.

Writing about the epitaphs composed in chequerboard style by the 6th/5th Century BC poet Simonides, Carson dismisses the notion that, in deciphering these letters, a kind of subjugation of the voice to the inscriptive process was involved.[82]

Carson, *Economy of the Unlost*, 84. note 28.

Stones inscribed in *scriptio continua*, or writing without gaps between the words, demanded to be read aloud; visual enigmas were unlocked aurally in their pronunciation - 'the verbs for "to read" in Greek typically begin with a prefix like *ana-* ("again") or *epi-* ("on top of") as if reading were essentially regarded as a sort of sympathetic vibration between letters composed by a writer and the voice in which the reader pulls them out of silence.'[83]

Carson, *Economy of the Unlost*, 84.

Anyone deciphering the *scriptio continua* used in the Sydney Olympics work *Relay* or *Nearamnew* can see that I aimed at the same re-entanglement of calligraphy and choreography. To decipher the sense of these public inscriptions, it is necessary to dawdle, to retrace tracks and explore different pathways; the act of deciphering materializes the meaning.

The return to ancient precedents lets me recapitulate, and clarify, another theme that surfaces throughout these notes: the relationship between writing and printing. Writing we will call a carving technique – etymologically, it involves scratching or incising - while the stamp of the glyph or font is the expression of a moulding technique. The impulse recorded in *Neglected Dimensions* has been, however, to fuse these contrasted attitudes towards the material. Bunjil's *Ber-rang* provides a mythological point of reference for a drawing practice that is erosive: it is impossible to say where a meaning had been scratched into the surface or impressed there. Perhaps ultimately we are revisiting in drawing rival theories of energy propagation and intuitively reconciling particle and wave models of movement. In any case, the fusion that occurs, however untutored and unrationalised its origin, is not simply a pragmatic concealment of poor *techne*: it opens up the possibility that the world is *letters all the way down*.

Writing presupposes the material of the world (into whose surfaces it scratches its calligraphy); printing, on the other hand, treats the ground like mud, as something that can be sculpted into shape. As 'The Artist's Vision' states in *Nearamnew*, with reference to surviving knowledge of Aboriginal cultures, 'If the shallows can supply such inestimable stones what may not the deep have held.'[84] Carter, *Mythform*, 98.   In the context of designing a typographic landscape, then, one is writing into writing: the act of writing fuses with sculpting. Letters serve as objects to be inscribed;

they can be hollowed out;
they can even be carved into landscapes (PLATE 44).

Equally, the writing that is responsible for hollowing out the
typographic matrix is not subordinated to conventions of sign
presentation and ordering that make writing legible; rewriting
certain passages,

> deepening them,

> gouging them out,

> as a cross-hatched sketch introduces chiaroscuro into the

form, it brings out the meaning (and new meanings) differently.

Referring to 'two fundamentally different techniques of
writing,' Bernhard Bischoff differentiates between the calligraphic
and the cursive. Constructed scripts, in which each letter is
individually designed and stands alone, are calligraphic. Upper case
or capital letters belong to this class. Cursive writing is different; its
components are drawn informally and stand together – in joined-up
writing, for example, the path of the stroke is entirely designed by the
logic of the ligatures binding the letters together. The cursive attaches
letters 'in a natural way to their neighbours.' Where ligatures lead
'by contraction of parts of the same or of different letters on the left
hand side, to a further freer rightward shift in the flow of the writing,'
the lean duplicates 'the forward motion of the walker
or the dancer.' [85]

Bernhard Bischoff, *Latin Paleography, Antiquity and the Middle Ages*, trans. D. Ó Cróinín & D. Ganz, Cambridge: Cambridge University Press, 1991, 51-52.

The contrast stated here could be an allegory of
public space writing where a feedback loop between
reading and treading is envisaged. The reader scoops out
space; tracks laid down in reading the script are cursive marks sculpting the architectural matrix into new forms. Frequently, within the
cursive labyrinth of the sketches, proto-architectural forms surface.
Amphitheatres stabilise in the whirling volutes PLATES 45,46; terraces,

the traditional milieu of the Muses, crystallise out of cellular jigsaws
or tight-stretched lattices (FIGS 16-19, 87).

89

These foreshadow the
fantasy played out in writing
public space. Out of the cursive
chaos arise capitals. The carving-
moulding operation generates
curvatures that nest inside themselves
the movement form. It produces cascades
of steps that three-dimensionalise the lines on the notebook
page (PLATE 42). Secreted in the upright *stoichos*, or ranged, upright
letter matrices may be ladders where the formal arrangement fissures
and new movements can be read (PLATE 45).

As scores of sociability, these rough sketches
reintroduce outwardness into writing. Fusing writing with drawing,
they draw out the repressed figural potential of lettering, the sense
in which it communicates visually – sometimes mimetically or
indexically. The means of turning writing inside out is the gesture and
the implied correspondence between the movement of the hand and
the movement of people in public space. Now public space gathers
people – the meeting place is an art of placing – but it also scatters:
in a recapitulation of Bunjil's second creation,
                    the artist-dramaturg of encounter embraces
a pre-history of approaching from a distance
and
    a post-history of
                dispersing.

Funnelled into the vortex of transformation, the turbulence
of the old involuted order is reformulated as a creative region
(PLATE 43). The *Ber-rang* cuts this way and that, Orphically-dissecting
the old tribal society and scattering their little bits across the land.
The gesture of scattering is, however, creative: like the elements
following their *ichnoi*, or tracks, in Plato's account of creation,[86]
Bunjil's Empedoclean crowd, jumbled,

> miscegenated and

> lost, miraculously reconstitutes itself

and the men and women find themselves allotted to their proper
places. The new society is inaugurated, an archipelago of related
communities, governed federally like the patchworked possum cloak.

A gesture of scattering was incorporated into the idea of Yagan
Square. 'When Noongar people visit a river or water body, we throw
a handful of sand into the water. We use language to let the Waugul
know of our presence. Noongar people see the condition of the rivers
and waterways as directly related to the wellbeing of Waugul. It is
part of our caring for country and the cultural landscape to ensure
that Waugul is not disturbed.'[87]
Waugul is the overarching spirit of the creative landscape and
responsible for all sources of life including the water, the seasons
and, in general their sustaining fertility.

In suggesting the foundation of Yagan Square in this gesture,
I wrote, 'The Yagan Square site is not given: it is premature to
talk about meeting. Permission to enter that place has yet to be
negotiated. Local trespasses, spirits and powers have to be addressed
and perhaps appeased. Certainly respect has to be shown. The custom
of casting a handful of sand into the water expresses this recognition.
It has a complex meaning. In a literal sense

it acknowledges

the powerful spirit

who made that waterway.

Sallis, *Chorology*, 127. See also Carter, *Dark Writing*, 96-99.

Kaartdijin Noongar/ Noongar Knowledge at https://www.noongarculture.org.au/spirituality.

It alerts him so that he
is not surprised; it offers him the opportunity to give a sign if the
trespass on his country is not welcome. In another, post-invasion
sense, it suggests the fragility of the ground, the paradox of ground
given or ceded and violently thrown away. It also suggests sharing,
giving and self-sacrifice. It is associated with the fundamental gesture
of amity, the opening of the palm to another. The gesture has
Indigenous meanings and ritual associations that are "inner";
the "outer" senses that can be shared include those of casting lots,
for the pattern the sand grains form as they are scattered
on the water is always different.'[88] Paul Carter, 'Creative Template at Yagan Square, Perth,' 2014, 1-11, 11. Unpublished.

Transposed to the choreography of public space, the gesture
of scattering draws attention to the prior condition of writing (and
reading) usually glossed over in western thought. Martin Heidegger
hints at this prior condition when he reflects, 'The essential
correlation
of the hand and the word ... is revealed in the fact that the hand
indicates and by indicating discloses what was concealed and therefore marks off, and while marking off forms the indicating marks into
formations. These formations are called, following the "verb" *graphein,*
grammata.'[89] Martin Heidegger, *Parmenides*, trans. R. Rojcewicz, A. Schuwer, Bloomington: Indiana University Press, 84.
In this meditation, a double movement implicit in
writing is retained: the hand that writes *indicates* or points out;
its power to disclose what lies scattered and unordered signifies
a differentiation or bringing to sense that, in a counter-movement,
draws together what has been disclosed. 'We call the disclosive
taking up and perceiving of the written word "reading" or "lection"
["*Lesen*"], i.e., col-lection, gathering – "'gleaning" ["*Ahren lessen*"],
in Greek *legein – logos.*'[90] Heidegger, *Parmenides*, 84.

In a fused writing/drawing practice, and in the place-making tradition it might describe, the double movement is no longer a push and pull between antithetical impulses. Like the string figure or a web of waves, it integrates a gesture of holding apart with an invitation to come over; a chiasmatic figure in the double sense of holding together and splitting apart, it imagines the construction of sociability in the flux. The serpentine power of Waugul is at once river and wind, the *bidi*, or blood path of the vein. It is also *waullu*, the paradox of the parting that joins. PLATE 33 meditates on these themes. The passenger who emerges from this negotiated passage must retain traces of the diffraction patterns created where the sand grains dotted their water. Initially, they may be little more than volumes beginning to take shape in the eddying wake. Later, the ghosts stalking the water generate fertile elemental involutes of their own that serve at last to entangle what has been so carefully approached and divided (PLATE 34).

12.

One drawing

practice from my youth,

which I failed to mention before, is *ballistic*, stemming from the aesthetic appeal of ball games. Playing a team sport such as football or hockey, the successful player sees doubly. There is the passage tunneled out by the flight of the ball, but there is also the mass movement, the trembling string figure of all the players in movement and the constantly altering arrangement of places they are opening up and closing. The drama of the game consists in the triumph of the time of *kairos* over the time of *chronos*; the endless interweave of chance and opportunity, of holes in space and the needles of flight that thread them, completely suspends the ordinary regulation of human behaviour according to rules of fixed position, untenanted interval and hierarchical succession.

A drawing of this situation is a drawing out of all the possibilities, as every passage,

        each arcing line,

        performed by the ball, depends for its sense-making on the fabric of other passages forming and unforming in its wake. A memory image of the game does not strictly draw one line over another but deepens our awareness of the patterning complexity; certainly, a chiaroscuro contrast between regions is likely, as more powerful trajectories prevail, but to the end outlying corners, as well as already densely traversed patches, communicate with one another: as the field of all possible encounters, they remain interrelated.

A further wonder of teams sports is that their appeal can be felt by the on-looker. The active creation, constant dismembering and re-membering of the movement form that the player experiences, can be identified and contemplated from afar. Long before the existence of 'mirror neurons' was posited, crowds attending football matches or baseball games intuitively linked vision to tactility, possessing an 'action understanding' that recognizes 'the intentions that underlie action'[91]: the action of the sports stadium may come as close as is empirically possible to illustrating Edmund Husserl's notion of consciousness as consciousness *of something*; both player and spectator are involved in an experience of directed awareness, or intentional consciousness, that embodies the etymological roots of the Latin *intendere* in the image of an arrow arcing or tending towards its moving target.[92]

The doodles of *Neglected Dimensions* can be compared to representations of the relational space and time of the game; they suggest the dynamics of a Spielraum that has no other purpose than its own weaving; as sketches for a dramaturgy of public space, they insist on the possibility of being simultaneously inside and outside the public movement form, a proposition that depends on liberating seeing from its imprisoning identification with the fixed point of view and reinserting it into the crowd of moving sensations where it projects itself into the lives and paths of other bodies.

At the same time, the steady state of the game's mass movement form is eventful: goals are scored or runs made, while within the general to and fro of the game, the pace and density of the action fluctuates. Comparably, a dramaturgy of public space drives towards the drama of possible meetings, and presupposes participants who are also desirous – demanding of communication with others. A primary sociality coexists with a sense of separateness; and without this double perspective, the play of sociability would have

Laura Elrick, 'Poetry, Ecology, and the Reappropriation of Lived Space,' *The Brooklyn Rail*. At http://www.brooklynrail.org/2006/06/poetry/poetry-ecology-and-the-reappropriation-of-lived-space

See Paul Carter, *The Lie of the Land*, London: Faber & Faber, 1996, 329.

no interest – rather literally, if we understand interest as the realm of
the *inter esse*, the interpersonal environment inhabited by all the paths
of propinquity. Without a sense of apartness, there would be no
impulse to become a part of the whole; equally, in the labyrinth
of identifications, paths must lead out into the solitary.

This connection between inflection and reflection – between
a bending towards (connected with the idea of intention) and an act
of self-conscious standing back that evaluates the character of what
is happening – is an ancient one. When I was reading the lives
of the athletes in preparation for writing the words of *Relay*, I was
struck by the description of Australian athlete Betty Cuthbert's
'agony' as she struggled with breathlessness to win the 200 metre title
in the 1956 Melbourne Olympics.[93] Carter, *Dark Writing*, 216.
It recalled classical metaphors
of athletes as types of the human soul, their race as an image of life's
race and their victory as an allegory of virtue's triumph over
circumstance. Similarly, drawing on a Greco-Roman tradition
of identifying intellectual and physical exertion, St Paul writes
of the *agon* of martyrdom. It is no accident that 'the more important
gymnasia, for example the Lyceum and the Academy, also became
centres of intellectual training and philosophy.'[94] Victor C. Pfitzner, *Strength in Weakness: a commentary on 2 Corinthians*, Adelaide: Lutheran Publishing House, c.1992, 23.

The place of meeting is the work of self-transcendence. In the
words of Betty Cuthbert: 'Time there.

> Me here.
>
> Never.
>
> Same.
>
> Me.
>
> Again.
>
> Ever a gain.
>
> Inside me riderless beat his hooves.'[95] Carter, *Dark Writing*, 216.

The event, the self-transcending moment that cannot be repeated,
does not simply evaporate: it takes its place in a history of improved
performances, where repetition consists in outstripping what went

before.

It could be an allegory for understanding the past differently.
Attending to the poetry of the race, and its history of dialogue
between limbs, out of which a different ground is named, experienced
and inhabited, a new understanding of meeting can be made. To go
over the track again is not to engage in Black Armband history,
however justified that may be, but, by finding a different way of
footing the course, to avoid stumbling and falling.
A competition to stay where you are without demanding exclusive
possession replaces a tradition of exposure,

expulsion and

erasure.

This insight, which obviously resembles such other formulations
as the chiasm, the self-departing moment of ecstasies (which also
produces a reunification) also articulates the structure, if you like,
of a history conceived in terms of the instants
between two strides, or of a geography written for
those in flight. It was interesting in this regard that, when I came
to study the signatures (often accompanied by identifying
monograms) of the Olympian athletes, I found myself going back
to older, and mostly discredited systems of graphic analysis. It was
old German techniques used in characterology and graphology that
seemed to suggest the character of these marks, and the sense in
which they were sketches of perpetual landing places.

At scale, the monograms operated like cartoons and were deployed
wittily – swimmers using amphibious imagery, while the jumpers and
sailors favoured cloud patterns – yet the signatures signified perhaps
nothing but the author's style. However, when enlarged, both
monogram and signature became apprehensible as something else,
miniatures of movement forms, indexical evocations of passage –

arcs,

trajectories and

measures.

A direct analogy seemed to exist between the drawing practice –
the manual labour involved in creating the distinctive outline – and
the athlete's career, understood here literally as the path of running,

sailing,

throwing

or

leaping.

They were characterological not in a psychological but in a kinetic
sense. Their *cursive* character directly related to the muscle memory
of the athlete – and to the *course* of the competition.

If the doodles collected in *Neglected Dimensions* represent
a dramaturgy of public space, they function in the same way.
The athletics of everyday life occurs under the aegis of *Ber-rang*
as the walker divides space and cleaves to the distance; it also
consists of the rebounding medium and the reverberations dying
away to nothing only to be renewed. It is the recognition and care
of these kinesthetic atmospheres that are sketched. Evidently, the
public space opened up in this way is neither the nowhere space of
contemporary urban planning nor the phantasm of the democratic
imagination. It is always a situated practice of self-becoming at that
place. The challenge is to represent it without fixing it, and,
in relation to onerous regimes of exclusion, to insist on its mobile,
refugee status. The object is not to define edges, but
instead to extend edges

every

where.

Projects referred to in text.

Dates refer to period of engagement.

Realised

Nearamnew, public art (ground pattern with nine script arrangements),
Federation Square, Melbourne.
> A collaboration with Lab architecture studio. 1998-2002.

Relay, public art (etched inscriptions and graffiti monograms), Sydney Olympics,
Fig Tree Grove, Homebush Bay, New South Wales.
> A collaboration with Ruark Lewis. 2000.

Zipcode, pedestrian passage design (ground pattern, stencilled glass, script designs)
Smith Street East, Darwin.
> By Material Thinking. 2008-2011.

Alterations, public art (ground pattern, etched inscription), Harmony Square,
Dandenong, Victoria.
> By Material Thinking. 2013.

Kelp, graphic animation, 'Hidden Histories', Warrnambool Art Gallery,
Warrnambool, Victoria.
> By Material Thinking, with Christopher Williams. April 2014.

Passenger, public art in seven parts (stencilled typography,
monumental sculptures), Yagan Square, Perth.
> By Material Thinking. 2016-2018.

Mystic Edge, public art (bi-lingual ground inscription and landscape form),
Scarborough Foreshore, Western Australia.
> By Material Thinking and Neville Collard,
> in association with landscape architects Taylor, Lethlean, Cullity. 2016-2017.

Unrealised

Tribute, Riverside Park landscape design proposed as a collaboration with landscape
architects Karres en Brands, Federation Square, Melbourne. 1998.

Tracks, design concept for public art (ground pattern, LED sculptures)
North Terrace Precinct, Adelaide (landscape architects Taylor, Lethlean, Cullity).
1999-2003.

Solution, public space design proposal, Victoria Harbour, Melbourne.
Client: Lendlease Group. 2002

Overflow, proposal for public art, Geelong Waterfront (landscape architects Taylor,
Lethlean, Cullity). 2000.

Botanic Gardens of Adelaide masterplan, concept sketch for landscape architects Taylor,
Lethlean, Cullity. 2003.

Pearl, landscape and public building design concept, Darwin Waterfront.
By Material Thinking. Client: Darwin Waterfront Corporation. 2008-2009.

Red Ways, urban design and integrated public art design concept, Alice Springs.
By Material Thinking. Client: Department of Planning and Infrastructure,
Northern Territory. 2007-2010.

Hamlet's Mill, public art proposal for 2012 Cultural Olympiad (London).
By Material Thinking. 2007-2009.

Biographies

Paul Carter is a UK-born cultural historian, radiophonic/installation composer and public artist. He migrated to Melbourne, Australia, in the early 1980s, where his reputation was established with the publication of *The Road to Botany Bay, an essay in spatial history* (1987, 2010). After publication of *Material Thinking, the theory and practice of creative research* (2004), he established a design studio of the same name with his son. The postcolonial poetics and politics of projects emerging from that studio are discussed in two publications, *Dark Writing, geography, performance, design* (2008) and *Places Made After Their Stories: design and the art of choreotopography* (2015). In 2020, Performance Research Books published *Absolute Rhythm*, works for minor radio. Productions of the ten scripts featured can be accessed and down-loaded from http://performance-research.org/absolute-rhythm. html. Artem (Naples) recently published Paul's artist's book, *Return of the Centaurs, a Field Guide* (2024). Paul is on the advisory boards of the journals *Drawing Matters* (Edinburgh) and *Estetica* (Naples). He is Professor of Design (Urbanism), School of Architecture and Urban Design, RMIT University, Melbourne.

John Warwicker is an artist, designer, and educator now based in Melbourne, Australia. He is a co-founder and continuing member of the creative collective 'tomato' in London and a Royal Designer for Industry (UK), a Fellow of the Royal Society of the Arts (UK), Professor of Graphic Design, at the Victorian College of the Arts VCA, University of Melbourne, and visiting Professor at Tokyo Zokei University and the Kuwasawa Design School. After obtaining a Master's degree in 'Electronic Interactive Media' (1981) he became the video dj for the band 'Freur', who later evolved into the influential dance band 'Underworld'. He describes his practice as 'Thought into Form by means of Language, irrelevant of medium or media, at any scale, for any duration, placed within the world'. Amongst the numerous awards he has won the prestigous Tokyo Type Directors special prize twice; first for his monograph *The Floating World*; then, in 2016, for the design of *O tomato Parco*, the multi-media exhibition in Parco and the streets of Shibuya, Tokyo.

Neglected Dimensions
Rough Sketches for Public Space

Published by
Actar Publishers, New York, Barcelona
www.actar.com

Author: Paul Carter

Illustrated by Paul Carter
Graphic Design by John Warwicker

Printing and binding
Grafiques Jou, Barcelona

Distribution
Actar D, Inc. New York, Barcelona.

New York
440 Park Avenue South, 17th Floor
New York, NY 10016, USA
T +1 2129662207
salesnewyork@actar-d.com

Barcelona
Roca i Batlle 2
08023 Barcelona, Spain
T +34 933 282 183
eurosales@actar-d.com

Indexing
English ISBN: 978-1-63840-160-5
Library of Congress Control Number: 2024941592

Printed in Spain

Publication date: 2025